How to use this book for your best advantange.

In the first section of the book, look for the answers to these provocative questions ...

- What • When • Where • Why • Which & • How?

to use each Sulky Stabilizer, Sulky Puffy Foam and Sulky KK 2000 Temporary Spray Adhesive to achieve professional-looking results in all of your creative projects.

To spark more creative uses for the stabilizers, we have included a "Quick Photo Reference" to projects using a particular stabilizer that you will find in 8 previously published *Concepts in Sulky Books* by various designers.

Following that is a special section to help you understand all of the elements involved in Successful Computerized Embroidery.

In the largest section, look for exciting, stimulating, creative Projects & Tips utilizing individual and combined Sulky Stabilizers, Puffy Foam and KK 2000.

Notice the colored tab references for finding your favorite stabilizer.

In the last section, you will find an Index and Sources for hard-to-find patterns, notions, etc. used in the projects. *Plus a Bonus pullout Multi-sized Vest Pattern.*

Introduction to the Sulky® Secrets to Successful Stabilizing!

by Joyce Drexler

• What are Stabilizers?

To those who have used stabilizers, they are a magic cure-all! They make the end result of all of our creative machine work look professional so we can achieve the great look we desired when we conceived the project. Sulky Stabilizers, except for Heat-Away, are all non-woven so they don't stretch in any direction and they don't dull your needle like paper products can. They are available as permanent cut-aways or temporary tear-aways; some are water soluble or heat-disintegrating.

• When do we use Stabilizers?

As you stitch on the huge range of fabrics available today, you will get a more professional result in virtually every creative project by using the right Sulky stabilizer or combination of stabilizers.

• Where do we use Stabilizers?

Stabilizers are traditionally used underneath the project as "backings" to support embroidery or any layering of thread on fabric. Some stabilizers are also used as "toppings" on top of the fabric being embellished.

• Why do we use Stabilizers in general?

We use "backing" stabilizers to relieve the stress placed on the fabric being embellished; they reduce or eliminate puckering, tunneling, or other unwanted reactions. Some can be used alone as the foundation on which our creative machine work is done.

We use "topping" stabilizers to help hold down the nap of some fabrics, to keep stitches from sinking into some fabrics, to enchance the clarity of fine lettering and detail stitching, or as a pattern, stencil or template to follow when stitching or painting.

Why use Sulky Stabilizers in particular?

Sulky stabilizers are carefully and thoughtfully engineered to enhance every creative project and solve even the most difficult problems. They are made of the highest quality materials, and quality is extremely important since inexpensive, poor quality stabilizers can sometimes cause poor registration of embroidery and premature tearing, among other problems.

• Which Stabilizers do we use?

Be sure that the stabilizers you use allow garments to move and bend

Meet the Author and read on to learn the secrets . . .

Joyce Drexler

Machine Artist, Quilter, Author, Designer, Creative Director and a Co-Managing Partner of Sulky of America as well as Co-Owner of Speed Stitch, Inc. from Port Charlotte, FL

Joyce is widely recognized as a leader in the field of "Machine Arts and Crafts". Since 1979 she has created over 200 products for her SPEED STITCH COMPANY in Florida. She has taught several thousand Retailers and Free Lance Teachers in Instructor Training Workshops across America and Canada. Her first book, "THREAD PAINTING" is in its 7th printing and has inspired hundreds of thousands of people to create works of machine art using her revolutionary simplified techniques. For nine years she successfully coordinated an annual national Retreat for sewers called "SMART". Joyce has taught at numerous Sewing Machine Company Conventions and Trade Shows over her 19 year career in the Sewing Industry.

The books Joyce has written have sold well over 300,000 copies and are being sold internationally. She is the producer and co-author of the Sulky Book Series "CONCEPTS IN SULKY" and she has written instructions for the Sulky Iron-on Transfer Pens and 9 Sulky Stabilizers.

Joyce has been published in numerous magazines, and she appears regularly on the PBS TV Programs: SEW CREATIVE; AMERICA SEWS WITH SUE HAUSMANN; CREATIVE LIVING; SEW PERFECT; QUILTING IN THE HEARTLAND; and KAYE'S QUILTING FRIENDS. She designed a one-of-a-kind garment for the prestigious Fairfield Fashion Show.

Joyce also creates the projects for SEW EXCITING SEMINARS and SULKY INSTRUCTOR TRAINING SEMINARS, and collaborates with Patsy Shields to teach the Sulky Educators that travel nationally conducting these Seminars. She also coordinates the Annual Sulky Challenge.

when the wearer does, while providing sufficient stability to stitch a high quality embroidered design or creative technique on the fabric.

Depending on the project, we will choose a stabilizer that may be placed either in the hoop, under the hoop, or stuck to the hoop; it may be ironed on, pinned in place, or adhered with Sulky KK 2000 Temporary Spray Adhesive. You'll know when you have the right stabilizer topping or backing because stitches lie perfectly without sinking into the fabric, all parts of the design or project are positioned perfectly because the fabric doesn't slip during stitching, and your stitched project doesn't sag, pull or pucker. To achieve that, this book will help you sort out which stabilizer or combination of stabilizers to choose.

• How do we use Stabilizers?

This is what you will learn in this book from the numerous, diversified, creative projects and tips from over 50 well-known industry professionals. **We will be discussing practical applications and guidelines - not rules** - for usage. Use this book as a source of inspiration, reference and information. If you have more ideas that we haven't touched on, we would love to hear from you. Maybe your tip or idea can be included in our next - *Update on Successful Stabilizing Book.*

Write, Fax or E-Mail us:
SULKY OF AMERICA
CONSUMER RELATIONS
3113 Boardpoint Dr., Dept.SB
Harbor Heights, FL 33983
FAX: 941-743-4634
E-mail: sulkyofamerica@mindspring.com
Visit our **website:** www.sulky.com

A Beginner's Guide to Machine Techniques for which SULKY® STABILIZERS are used.

Technique	Heat-Away	Solvys	Tear-Easy	Stiffy	Totally Stable	Sticky	Cut-Away Plus	Cut-Away Soft 'n Sheer
Battenburg Lace	•	•						
Bias Tube Work	•	•						
Buttonholes	•	•	•					
Charted Needlework					•			
Computerized Embroidery	•	•	•	•	•	•	•	•
Couching Yarns	•	•	•	•	•	•		
Crazy Patchwork			•	•	•		•	
Cutwork	•	•	•					•
Decorative Stitching		•	•	•		•	•	•
Edges	•	•	•					
Fabric Applique	•	•	•		•		•	•
Fabric Print Embellishment	•	•	•		•			
Fagoting		•						
Foundation for Faux Paper Piecing Techniques		•	•					
Free-Motion Thread Painting	•	•	•	•				
Free-Standing Covered Cording		•						
Heirloom Sewing	•	•	•					
Liquid Stabilizing		•						
Metallizing Fabric with Sulky Metallic Threads	•	•	•					
Monogramming	•	•	•		•		•	•
Outline Satin Stitching	•	•	•		•			
Pattern Making			•	•	•	•		
Puffy Foam Embroidery/Applique			•	•	•	•	•	•
Serger Lace		•						
Shadow Work		•						
Smocking by Machine		•			•	•		
Stenciling				•				
Straight Stitch Writing	•	•						
Templates			•	•		•		•
Thread Spun Lace/Bobbin Lace	•	•						
3-D Fabric Applique		•						
3-D Free-Motion & 3-D ComputerEmbroidery	•	•						
Thread Sketching		•	•					
Transferring Designs		•	•					
Trapunto								•

You may still need to alter these recommendations for your specific machine.

Make any Stabilizer (except Heat-Away) a "Sticky-type" with Sulky KK 2000™ Temporary Spray Adhesive .

• What? • When? • Where? • Why? & • How? to Sucessfully use ...

Sulky Soft 'n Sheer™ & Cut-Away Plus™

What is a Cut-Away Stabilizer?

A "cut-away" stabilizer is a <u>non-woven, permanent</u> stabilizer that must be cut away to be removed. Cut-aways should never tear because, if they do, they are not giving you the needed stability for which you are using them. Soft 'n Sheer is an unusually fabricated non-woven similar to the lining found in disposable diapers. This textured stabilizer is very sheer and supple, yet almost impossible to tear, making it ideal for knits worn next to the skin. Cut-Away Plus is a mid-weight non-woven which is ideal for outerwear like sweaters, sweatshirts, and jackets.

When would I use a Cut-Away Stabilizer?

Soft 'n Sheer and Cut-Away Plus Stabilizers are recommended as backings to add stability to the embroidery of goods with a delicate hand where the embroidery can pull down or sag from the surrounding fabric if left to stand alone through washings and wearings; also, for dense embroidery designs, open-weave fabrics, or lightweight fabrics when stitching a complex design.

Where would I use a Cut-Away <u>Permanent</u> Stabilizer?

Use it when Machine Embroidering and Appliqueing on knits like T-shirts, Golf Shirts, Sweaters and Sweatshirts, Lycra Swimwear, Work-out and Bike Pants. Light and airy Soft 'n Sheer is especially good for clothing which is worn next to the skin; mid-weight Cut-Away Plus is ideal for outerwear.

Be sure to check out the projects featured in this book starting on page 46.

Why would I use a Sulky Cut-Away Stabilizer instead of another kind of Sulky Stabilizer?

When you want the <u>continued support of a stabilizer</u> for the thread area through wearing and laundering. <u>Tear-away's give temporary support</u> during the embellishing process only. While Tear-Away stabilizers are faster and easier to use, they have limited usefulness on unstable goods because each needle penetration diminishes their support. When a Tear-Away is perforated, it can be punched out, making it a poor choice for high stitch count designs, open weave fabrics, or lightweight fabrics with a complex design.

How would I use Cut-Away Stabilizers?

*   *One layer in a hoop, more under the hoop if needed for Computerized Machine Embroidery.*
*   *Use them with a ballpoint needle when stitching on knits and fine silk.*
*   *Use Soft 'n Sheer for Trapunto techniques.*
*   *Spray with Sulky KK 2000 Temporary Spray Adhesive to make into a "sticky-type" stabilizer to embroider small areas like collars, cuffs, pockets, etc. that aren't large enough to fit in a hoop.*
*   *When you are done stitching, carefully cut away excess stabilizer without cutting the fabric it is stabilizing. Trim close to the stitching to minimize stabilizer show-through on white or light colored fabrics.*

At-A-Glance ...
How to use Sulky
Cut-Away Plus™
& Soft 'n Sheer™
Permanent Stabilizers

1. Use as a Stabilizer Backing for Machine Embroidery, Applique and Monogramming ...

by placing *Cut-Away* in the hoop under the fabric design area to be stitched. For other non-hoop applications, pin, baste or spray Sulky KK 2000 Temporary Adhesive onto the material to adhere it to the Cut-Away. Ideal for woven or knit fabrics. Use one, two or three layers as needed.

2. Removal is Easy ...

once stitching is completed, remove from hoop, clip all loose bobbin threads, and cut away the stabilizer up to the outer edge of the stitching, leaving enough around the design to permanently support the stitching. **The stabilizer inside the stitched design also remains for permanent stability.** Press out hoop marks if there are any.

Try Sulky Cut-Away Plus on the convenient 7-2/3" personal roll or Soft 'n Sheer on the 8" roll for quick use, with minimal wastage, when doing computerized embroidery and monogramming. Both Cut-Aways are also available in one yard packages and by yardage on a bolt.

Fall in love with Cut-Away Stabilizers for Programmed Embroidery and Applique Work

Depending on the density of your fabric and embroidery design, you may need to use one to three layers of a Sulky Cut-Away. Do a test to determine what set-up works best for the combination of fabric and embroidery design or applique that you are working with. Place one layer of *Cut-Away* in the hoop under the fabric, and spray Sulky KK 2000 on any additional needed layers and slide them under the hoop. Or try adhering Sulky Sticky to the back of the hoop, then placing the Cut-Away under the hoop to create a more permanent situation for support during laundering that will also feel reasonably soft next to your skin.

Unstable goods require a Cut-Away as do some stable goods onto which a high stitch count design will be stitched, but it doesn't always provide crisp resolution of fine column (satin) stitching like small lettering. You can enhance the clarity and resolution by using Sulky Stiffy Tear-Away as a bottom backing under the hoop (next to the machine) combined with a Cut-Away in the hoop.

· What? · When? · Where? · Why? & · How? to Sucessfully use ...

Sulky Heat-Away™

What is Heat-Away Stabilizer?

Heat-Away is a heat disintegrating *Temporary* Stabilizer. Once your project is stitched, simply adjust your iron or ironing press to the temperature for linen (no steam, approximately 430°F). Protect your ironing surface from the ash with a teflon press cloth or brown bag. Protect delicate fabrics and uncoated irons with a press cloth between the Heat-Away and the iron. Iron (press) on the garment for 10-15 seconds, moving the iron slightly to compensate for steam holes, until the Heat-Away turns brown. Gently brush away the ash with a soft bristle brush (like an old soft toothbrush). If making Needle Lace, place in a zip-lock bag to catch the ash and gently massage to remove the Heat-Away from the stitching. **NEVER, NEVER EXPOSE TO LIQUIDS until all of the Heat-Away has been disintegrated. Any liquid will loosen the chemical that causes Heat-Away to disintegrate, allowing it to travel into your thread or fabric, making it disintegrate as well when a hot iron is applied.**

When would I use Heat-Away Stabilizer?

In cases where I normally would use a removable water soluble Stabilizer like Sulky Solvy that does not require tearing, but <u>when water removal is not an option.</u> For techniques requiring a firm, fabric-like foundation. Do not use on fabrics or with fibers that can't tolerate the heat necessary to disintegrate Heat-Away.

Where would I use Heat-Away Stabilizer?

Use it as a "topper" in machine embroidery or buttonholes when a water soluble stabilizer can not be used --- such as on velvet and velveteen, and any dry cleanable fabric that has a nap. Some Wearable Art Designers use it for Battenburg Lace and as a foundation for special free-motion work like Machine Spun Lace (Needlelace), Bobbin Lace, and Faux Weaving by Machine. It's great to use as "the fabric" when making computerized embroidery motifs into "fabric-free" pins, magnets, etc.

Be sure to check out the projects featured in this book starting on page 51 and all of the projects that feature Sulky Heat-Away in past Concepts in Sulky Books.

Why would I use Heat-Away instead of another kind of Sulky Stabilizer?

When you don't want to run the risk of either tearing out threads, having a permanent cut-away showing or when water removal is prohibited.

How would I use and store Heat-Away Stabilizer?

- *In a hoop for computerized machine embroidery.*
- *By itself (not in a hoop) for some Needlelace, Faux Woven Projects and Edgework.*
- *On top of the fabric when a nap needs to be held down for embroidery or monogramming on a fabric that can not receive water as a removal method.*
- *Use a craft embossing or heat gun to remove Heat-Away "pokies".*
- *To protect the ironing surface, place a teflon pressing sheet or press cloth on the fabric before burning off the Heat-Away.*
- *Always cut away as much of the excess Heat-Away before applying the iron for removal.*
- *Heat-Away must be protected against moisture, heat and sun --- store unused portions in a sealed zip-lock bag.*
- *Embroidered designs where Heat-Away is not removed at once should also be stored in a sealed zip-lock plastic bag.*

At-A-Glance ...
How to use Sulky Heat-Away™
disintegrating brush-off
Stabilizer.

1. To Trace or Transfer ...

design onto Heat-Away, place permanent pattern under Heat-Away, then trace it with an extra-fine, permanent-ink marker. Use Heat-Away as a design template to stitch through or as a pattern guide and stitching support piece as in 3-D Applique, Spun Lace, Battenburg Lace, etc.

Perfect for any project where wetting or tearing would cause distortion to stitches or damage to your base material.

2. Use as a Stabilizer ...

by placing Heat-Away under or over fabric or design area to be stitched (no hoop needed). You may pin or baste material to it if desired. Do not use on fabrics or with fibers that can't tolerate the heat necessary to disintegrate Heat-Away.

Try Sulky Heat-Away on the convenient 8" wide personal roll for quick use, with minimal wastage, when doing computerized machine embroidery and monogramming. It is also available by yardage on a bolt and in 15" x 22" packages.

Never, never expose to liquids until all of the Heat-Away has been disintegrated.

Any liquid will loosen the chemical that causes Heat-Away to disintegrate, allowing it to travel into your thread or fabric, making it disintegrate as well when a hot iron is applied.

3. Removal is Easy ...

once stitching is completed, disintegrate Heat-Away by placing a dry, hot iron (cotton or linen setting) on it until it turns brown - about 10 to 15 seconds. Gently brush away brown Heat-Away with a soft bristle brush like a toothbrush. For delicate fabrics, try a lower heat setting for a slightly longer time. Always test heat setting on a sample piece of material. Protect delicate fabrics, decorative threads (Rayons, Metallics, etc.) and uncoated irons with a press cloth between Heat-Away and iron.

Quick Reference:
Heat-Away
Step-by-Step Projects found in the Concepts in Sulky Book Series

"Dimensional Thread Applique"
by Janet Puluch, p. 20-23,
Embellishing Concepts in
Sulky Book 900B8 ▶

"Spinning Sulky Lace
by Machine" by Sharee Dawn
Roberts, p. 37-39,
Embellishing Concepts
in Sulky Book 900B8 ▶

"Couching Nubby
Decorative Yarns"
Sulky Texturized Vest
◀ *by Kathy Stachowicz, p. 7,*
Patchwork Concepts
in Sulky Book 900B9

"Sulky Fiber Pin"
by Joyce Drexler and
Patsy Shields, p. 20 & 21, ▶
Patchwork Concepts
in Sulky Book 900B9

"Magic Windows Vest"
techniques by Ginny Jahnke
◀ *Sample Vest by* ▶
Cynthia Brawn.
p. 36-40,
Patchwork Concepts
in Sulky Book 900B9

• What? • When? • Where? • Why? & • How? to Sucessfully use ...

Sulky Solvy™ *and* Super Solvy™

What are Solvy and Super Solvy Stabilizers?

They are Water Soluble, **Temporary** *Stabilizers or transfer agents that are made of a polyvinyl alcohol film so they dissolve in water like magic!* **Super Solvy is twice as thick, heavy and strong as the Original Sulky Solvy!** *Both are non-toxic and resistant to organic materials such as fats, oils, etc. They will dissolve in water with a temperature of anywhere from 32° to 200°. To make either type thicker and firmer, two or more layers can be fused together by applying a hot iron for several seconds.*

When would I use Solvy and/or Super Solvy Stabilizer?

Both types are perfect as a topper on napped fabrics like towels to keep the loops or piles from poking through stitching, to prevent stitches from getting lost in the fabric, and to enhance the clarity of fine lettering and detail stitching. Make Solvy into a **liquid stabilizer** *by dissolving 1 yard (1/2 yard of Super Solvy) in 8 oz. of water. Brush liquid Solvy onto flimsy or sheer fabrics that are to be stitched. Do not use it on non-washable fabrics like velvet or silk.*

Where would I use Solvy and/or Super Solvy Stabilizer?

Use it anywhere that dissolving the stabilizer would be preferable to tearing, cutting or heating it away. Both are widely used in the following techniques:
- *Quilting • Embroidery • Lace Work • Buttonholes • Thread Sketching*
- *As a time-saving substitute for Paper in Foundation Piecing • Edgework*
- *Charted Needlework Design Patterns • Intricate Embroidery Designs on Knitwear*
- *Cut Work • Monogramming • Machine Spun Lace (Needlelace) • 3-D Applique*
- *Shadow Work • Heirloom Serging and Sewing • Battenburg Lace • Smocking*
- *Lightweight and Sheer Fabrics • Toweling • Hand-turned Applique*
- *Serger Lace*

Be sure to check out the projects featured in this book starting on page 67 and all of the projects that feature Solvy and Super Solvy in past Concepts in Sulky Books.

Why would I use Solvy and/or Super Solvy Stabilizer instead of another kind of Sulky Stabilizer?

Both Solvys allow us to:
1. *Stitch with a delicate straight stitch or on delicate fabrics without concern that the stitching will be pulled out or distorted when the stabilizer is removed.*
2. *Leave no "fuzzy" white edges when removed.*
3. *Iron layers together for heavier treatments.*
4. *Add no bulk to designs.*
5. *Make a liquid stabilizer from scraps left over from other projects ... No Waste!*
6. *Write, draw, trace or transfer onto them with either a permanent-ink marker, Sulky Iron-On Transfer Pen, or a water soluble marker.*

How would I use and store Solvy and/or Super Solvy Stabilizer?

Either can be used in a hoop by itself, above the fabric as a topper, under the fabric as a stabilizer, or ironed together in layers to stand alone. Trace, draw or transfer a design onto Solvy, then spray Sulky KK 2000 Temporary Spray Adhesive onto the fabric, and hand press Solvy to the fabric for a pattern to follow when Quilting or Thread Sketching. Store unused portions in a sealed zip-lock bag. Store unused liquid Solvy in a sealed, marked jar in your refrigerator.

Quick steps to using Sulky Solvy™ & Super Solvy™ *Water Soluble* Stabilizers.

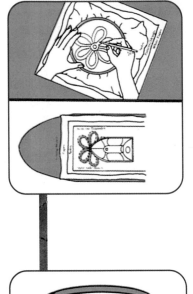

1. To Trace or Transfer ...

a design onto either Solvy, place the design under the Solvy (secured in a hoop for handling ease) and trace it with an extra-fine, permanent-ink marker or a washout or disappearing ink marker depending on color of thread and fabric to be used. Iron-on transfers can be ironed onto Solvy with a dry iron (NO STEAM).

Use as a design template to stitch through to transfer a design onto fabric as in Quilting, Monogramming, Thread Sketching and Lace Making, or as a pattern guide and stitching support piece to do Cut-Work, Battenburg Lace, Fagoting, 3-D Applique, Machine Beading and Shadow Work Applique.

2. Use as a Stabilizer ...

under fabric or design area to be stitched by either adhering with Sulky KK 2000, securing in a hoop, or ironing, basting or pinning one to three layers in place. Use as a hooped topping on napped materials like terry cloth to prevent stitches from sinking into the fabric and to keep the loops or pile from poking through the stitching.

Solvy as a fusible... Spray fabric with Sulky KK 2000 Temporary Spray Adhesive, then finger-press Solvy onto the fabric. **Solvy as a liquid ...** brush it on as a liquid stabilizer made by dissolving 1 yd. (1/2 yard of Super Solvy) in 8 oz. of water. **Layers of Solvy can be pressed together ...** to make either type firmer or heavier, two or more layers can be fused together by applying a hot, dry iron for several seconds; cover with a press cloth if your iron does not have a non-stick surface. Use with or without a hoop.

Try Sulky Solvy and Super Solvy on the convenient 8" wide personal roll for quick use, with minimal wastage, when doing computerized embroidery and monogramming. Both are also available by yardage on a bolt and in 1 yard packages.

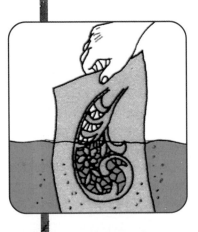

3. Removal is Easy ...

once stitching is completed, carefully trim or tear away excess Solvy, then put a damp press cloth on remaining Solvy. Any Solvy that remains can be removed by submerging project in cool water for 3-5 minutes. *Rinse thoroughly.* Air dry on a towel. It may take a little longer to dissolve Solvy that has been pressed together or when using Super Solvy.

Quick Reference
Solvy and Super Solvy Step-by-Step Projects found in the Concepts in Sulky Book Series

"3-D Ultra Suede Applique"
by Libby Tower, p. 3,
Concepts in Sulky Book 900B1

"Thread Sketching"
by Joyce Drexler, p. 5,
Concepts in Sulky Book 900B1

"Decorative Stitched Patches"
by Louise Baird, p. 25,
Elegant Concepts in Sulky
Book 900B4

"Scalloped-Edge Collar"
by Louise Baird, p. 6,
Elegant Concepts in Sulky
Book 900B4

"French Hand Sewn Cut Work
Christmas Stockings"
by Louise Baird, p. 8,
Elegant Concepts in Sulky
Book 900B4

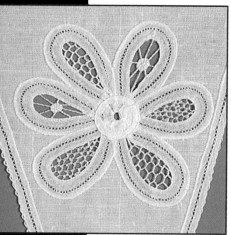

"Battenburg Lace"
by Louise Baird, p. 13
Elegant Concepts in Sulky
Book 900B4

"Cut Work Sweatshirt Yoke"
by Joyce Drexler
and Louise Baird, p. 23,
Elegant Concepts in Sulky
Book 900B4

"Cut Work and Shadow Work
Applique"
by Joyce Drexler and
Jane Hill, p. 27,
Concepts in Sulky Book 900B1

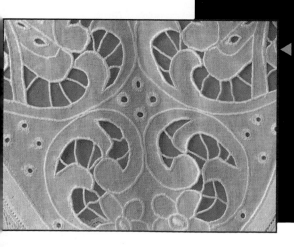

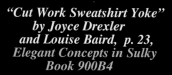

Quick Reference
Solvy and Super Solvy Projects found in the Concepts in Sulky Book Series

"Cutwork Applique Neckline"
Jeanie Adams, p. 16,
Surface Design
Concepts in Sulky Book 900B6

"Shaded Thread Applique"
by Libby Lehman, p. 20,
Surface Design Concepts
in Sulky Book 900B6

"Bias Tube Work"
by Louise Baird,
Inside Front Cover,
Elegant Concepts
in Sulky Book 900B4

"Thread Sketching"
by Joyce Drexler, p. 8,
Embellishing Concepts
in Sulky Book 900B8

"Angel Applique
Free-Motion Face"
by Ellen Osten, p. 13-16,
Embellishing Concepts
in Sulky Book 900B8

"Geometric Applique"
Janet O'Brien and
Debbie Garbers, p. 28-32,
Embellishing Concepts
in Sulky Book 900B8

"Grandma's Brag Vest"
by Pauline Salzman, p. 23-25,
Embellishing Concepts
in Sulky Book 900B8

"Embellished Fabric using
Liquid Solvy"
by Joyce Drexler, p. 12,
Surface Design Concepts
in Sulky Book 900B6

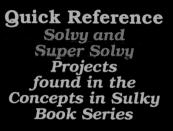

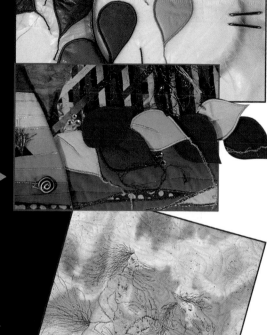

Quick Reference
Solvy and Super Solvy Projects found in the Concepts in Sulky Book Series

"3-D Embroidered Trees"
by Joyce Drexler, p. 10-12,
Patchwork Concepts
in Sulky Book 900B9

"3-D Appliqued Leaves"
by Ginny Jahnke, p. 19,
Patchwork Concepts
in Sulky Book 900B9

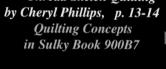

"Thread Sketch Quilting"
by Cheryl Phillips, p. 13-14
Quilting Concepts
in Sulky Book 900B7

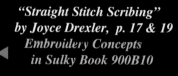

"Straight Stitch Scribing"
by Joyce Drexler, p. 17 & 19
Embroidery Concepts
in Sulky Book 900B10

"Sulky Covered Piping"
by Ann Boyce, p. 25,
Quilting Concepts
in Sulky Book 900B7

"Thread Sketched Background"
by Joyce Drexler, p. 15,
Embroidery Concepts
in Sulky Book 900B10

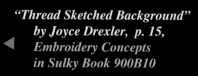

"3-D Thread Painted
Applique Flowers"
by Joyce Drexler, p. 32,
Embroidery Concepts
in Sulky Book 900B10

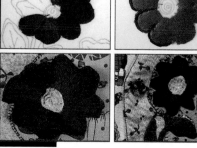

At a Glance, it's easy to use . . .

Sulky Tear-Easy™

for tracing, transferring and stabilizing.

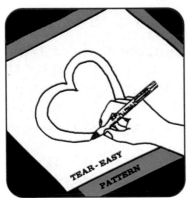

1. Trace . . .

design onto see-through Tear-Easy by placing a permanent pattern under Tear-Easy, then tracing it with an extra-fine, permanent-ink marker; or heat-transfer the design with a Sulky Iron-on Transfer Pen. Use Tear-Easy as a design template to stitch through or as a pattern guide and stitching support piece as in Monogramming or Programmed Machine Embroidery.

2. Use as a Stabilizer . . .

by placing Tear-Easy under or over fabric or design area to be stitched (hoop optional). You may pin, baste or temporarily adhere material to it by spraying Sulky KK-2000 onto it. For added support on delicate fabrics, use two or more layers.

3. Removal is Easy . . .

once stitching is completed, gently tear away Tear-Easy one layer at a time to prevent the pulling, tearing or distorting of stitches that can occur when tearing away a single layer of a thicker, heavier stabilizer.

Sulky Stiffy™

for backing embroidery, monograms, appliques and other decorative applications.

1. Use as a Backing Stabilizer . . .

under fabrics or design area to be stitched: either secure Stiffy in a hoop, pin or temporarily adhere material to it by spraying Sulky KK-2000 onto it. Some professional embroiderers prefer to put one layer of Stiffy in the hoop and one or two layers sprayed with KK 2000 under the hoop before they begin stitching.

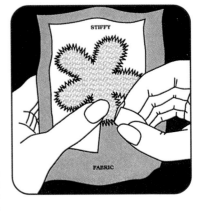

2. Removal is Easy . . .

once stitching is completed, gently tear away Stiffy. To prevent any pulling, tearing or distorting of stitches, hold the embroidery firmly in one hand while carefully tearing the Stiffy away from it one layer at a time, if you used 2 or more layers.

Generally, the thinner the woven fabric, the heavier your backing stabilizer or layers of a lighter weight stabilizer should be.

When additional layers are needed for computerized embroidery, once hoop is on machine, simply spray Sulky KK-2000 Temporary Spray Adhesive on each additional layer and slide it under the hoop.

Tear-Easy and Stiffy are both available in 1 yard packages, by yardage on bolts, and on convenient 8" personal rolls for quick use, with minimal wastage, when doing computerized embroidery. Use either Tear-Easy or Stiffy as a topping to achieve greater opacity or thread coverage in some programmed machine embroidery. A mostly white fill on a dark or black fabric can take fewer stitches by placing Tear-Easy or Stiffy on the goods in the hoop. After stitching the underlay, stop the machine, tear away excess, then complete the stitching.

• What? • When? • Where? • Why? & • How? to Sucessfully use ...
Sulky Tear-Easy™ & Stiffy™

What are Tear-Easy & Stiffy Stabilizers?

*Both are made of **non-woven** materials so they **don't stretch** in any direction, providing excellent stability through the stitching process, and they tear away easily in both directions once the stitching is completed.*

When would I use a Tear-Easy or Stiffy Stabilizer?

With few exceptions, even the most stunning design or surface embellishment won't work properly unless it is stitched over the right stabilizer backing that provides the stability needed to keep every stitch in place. Tear-aways are used under fabrics to prevent tunneling, distorting of stitches and puckering in techniques where removing the stabilizer by tearing will neither disturb the hand of the stitching, nor pull, distort or loosen the stitches on the edge of the design.

*Tear-Easy is a **soft, lightweight** temporary stabilizer that provides great stability as a backing, combined with effortless removal. It is used as a topping in quilting and as a foundation in paper-piecing. Stiffy is a **crisp, firm, medium weight**, temporary stabilizer that is used when a heavier tear-away is preferred.*

Where would I use Tear-Easy or Stiffy Stabilizer?

Use Tear-Easy or Stiffy as a backing for all types of Applique, Programmed and Free-motion Embroidery, Edge Stitching, Monogramming, Buttonholes and Decorative Stitching. See the Computerized Machine Embroidery Chart on page 34 for recommended use with certain fabric choices. Tear-Easy can be used as a quilting stitching pattern.

Be sure to check out the projects featured in this book starting on page 89 and all the projects that feature Tear-Easy and Stiffy in past Concepts in Sulky Books.

Why would I use Sulky Tear-Easy or Stiffy Stabilizer instead of another kind of Stabilizer?

Although thicker stabilizers may cost a little more, they can be more economical if you only need to use one piece versus several pieces of a thinner one. On the other hand, you can tie up a lot of money and spend a great deal of time experimenting with 5 or 6 weights each of 5 different types of stabilizers when virtually all of your stabilizer needs can be met by using the nine Sulky Stabilizers, with an occasional multi-layer application or combination of different Sulky Stabilizers. Ultra stiffness in a tear-away may provide the support you need, but if it pulls out stitches when torn away, it could ruin the project. That's when layering the softer, easier-to-tear Tear-Easy can be the right choice because you can easily tear away one layer at a time. When doing computerized embroidery, crisp, mid-weight Sulky Stiffy is well-suited to low stitch count patterns with fine detail. Clarity of column (satin) stitches is enhanced with Stiffy, and it is often used as a bottom backing under the hoop combined with Cut-Away Soft 'n Sheer in the hoop.

How would I use Tear-Easy or Stiffy Stabilizers?

One layer under the fabric in a hoop with 1-2 layers under the hoop if needed for Computerized Machine Embroidery, Applique and Monogramming. Always tear away one layer at a time. Spray them with Sulky KK 2000 to make either into a "sticky-type" backing stabilizer for embroidering small areas like collars, cuffs, pockets, etc. that aren't large enough to fit in a hoop. Use Tear-Easy as a topper for stitching quilting designs and as a foundation replacement for paper-piecing. Use Tear-Easy for supporting edges of garments for embellishing, topstitching and buttonholes.

◄ *"Embroidered*
Gardener's Vest"
by Bonnie Slinker, p. 42
Patchwork Concepts
in Sulky Book 900B9 ►

◄ *"Traditional Fabric Applique"*
by Ann Heitkamp, p. 3
Concepts in Sulky
Book 900B1

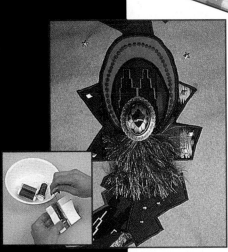

"Sulky Tassels" ►
by Ginny Jahnke
Front Inside Cover
Applique Concepts
in Sulky Book 900B3

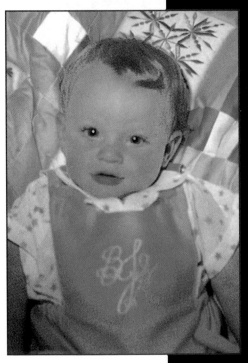

◄ *"Monogramming and*
Pictogram Designs"
by Dawn Wallerstedt Stark
p. 6 & 21
Concepts in
Sulky Book 900B1

"Strip-Pieced ►
Computerized Embroidered
Patchwork Vest"
by Joyce Drexler, p. 22
Patchwork Concepts in
Sulky Book 900B9

16

Quick Reference
Sulky Tear-Easy Stabilizer
Step-by-Step Projects found in the Concepts in Sulky Book Series

◄ *"Crazy Patchwork Embroidered Vest" by Sharon Stokes, p. 46 Patchwork Concepts in Sulky Book 900B9*

"Sulky Embroidered Christmas Patchwork Quilted Wallhanging" by Verna Erickson, p. 47 Patchwork Concepts in Sulky Book 900B9 ►

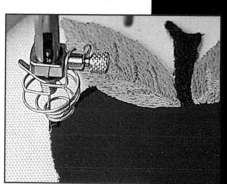

"Embroidered Quilt Design Patchwork Vest" by Patsy Shields, p. 43 Patchwork Concepts in Sulky Book 900B9 ◄

"Sulky Personalized Christmas Stocking" by Joyce Drexler, p. 48 Patchwork Concepts in Sulky Book 900B9 ►

◄ *"Free-Motion Embroidery" by Joyce Drexler, p. 2-6 Embroidery Concepts in Sulky Book 900B10*

"Sulky Elegant Dewdrops" by Jeanie Sexton, p. 9 Embroidery Concepts in Sulky Book 900B10 ►

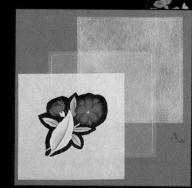

Quick Reference

Sulky Tear-Easy Stabilizer Step-by-Step Projects found in the Concepts in Sulky Book Series

"Sulky Twin-Needle Thread Painting" ▶
by Debbie McKee, p. 44-46
Embroidery Concepts in Sulky Book 900B10

◀ *"Random Fabric Weaving"*
by Joyce Drexler, p. 17
Embroidery Concepts in Sulky Book 900B10

◀ *"Sulky Thread Painted Daisy Appliques"*
by Joyce Drexler , p. 16
Embroidery Concepts in Sulky Book 900B10

"Scanner Sulky Embroidery Designs" ▶
by Jan Brashears, p. 12
Embroidery Concepts in Sulky Book 900B10

18

• What? • When? • Where? • Why? & • How? to Sucessfully use ...

Sulky Totally Stable™

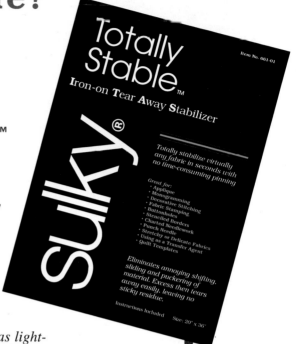

What is Sulky Totally Stable Iron-on Stabilizer?

Totally Stable is a non-woven, medium-weight, iron-on, temporary tear-away stabilizer. It is coated on one side so that it can be temporarily fused to a fabric to eliminate shifting, sliding, puckering and stretching of that fabric while it is being stitched. It is perfect for stretchy fabrics like knits.

When would I use Totally Stable Iron-on Stabilizer?

You would use Totally Stable for stabilizing stretch fabrics as well as lightweight wovens when the fabric is suitable for ironing. Not preferred for nylon or lycra. It can be re-ironed and used over and over until the fusible no longer adheres. It is perfect to make iron-on, reuseable design stitching templates.

Where would I use Totally Stable Iron-on Stabilizer?

Use it on knits like T-shirts, Golf Shirts, and Sweatshirts when Machine Embroidering, Monogramming and Appliqueing if a temporary tear-away stabilizer is preferred over a permanent one. It is perfect for supporting charted needlework by machine. Stencil Painters find Totally Stable ideal because you can see through it for easy tracing, it can be fan folded, and border stencils can be cut easily from it. It can be ironed onto fabric or a garment and act as the perfect stencil while applying stencil paint and it can be carefully removed and reapplied if a pressing sheet is used. It can also be used as a blocking agent when double stamping. It makes a great iron-on template for quilting and applique as well.

Be sure to check out the projects featured in this book starting on page 95 and all of the projects that feature Totally Stable in past Concepts in Sulky Books.

Why would I use Totally Stable Iron-on Stabilizer instead of another kind of Sulky Stabilizer?

When you need the fabric totally stabilized, no other stabilizer irons on in a temporary, reuseable manner like Sulky Totally Stable. By ironing Totally Stable onto a fabric, the fabric can not shift or stretch on the stabilizer, making it much easier to embellish or stitch on. Totally Stable is the only stabilizer that you can make into an iron-on template.

How would I use Totally Stable Iron-on Stabilizer?

- *Place the shiny, fusible side of the Totally Stable against the wrong side of the fabric and press for several seconds with a dry iron at a cotton setting using a steady, quick ironing motion. Once the project is completed, you can remove the Totally Stable and reuse it again and again.*
- *If multiple rehooping is required, the stabilizer may loosen and need to be ironed again to readhere it.*
- *Once the stitching is completed, Totally Stable peels up and tears away, leaving no residue.*
- *Do not iron Totally Stable onto fabric that has been marked with air or water soluble markers since the heat of the iron could set the ink, making your markings permanent.*

At-A-Glance ... it's easy to use Sulky Totally Stable™ *Temporary Iron-on Tear-Away Stabilizer.*

1. To Trace or Transfer ...

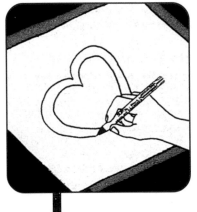

the design onto see-through *Totally Stable*, place the permanent pattern under *Totally Stable* and trace it with either an extra-fine, permanent-ink marker, a washout marker, or a disappearing ink marker. Then iron it onto the fabric, giving you a smooth, trouble-free design pattern to follow.

Designs drawn or traced with a Sulky Iron-on Transfer Pen can be ironed onto Totally Stable as you are adhering Totally Stable to your fabric or after Totally Stable has been pressed on.

Place the shiny, fusible side of Totally Stable against the wrong side of the fabric and press for 5 to 10 seconds with a dry iron at a cotton setting* using a steady, quick ironing motion, then check to see if the fusing is complete. If not, apply iron for several more seconds until Totally Stable is totally fused. You can use *Totally Stable as an iron-on, non-bleeding, temporary, reusable design template* to stitch around as in quilting, bobbin work, and upside-down applique. Or use it as a perfect *iron-on pattern guide and totally stable stitching support* piece as in Monogramming, Programmed Machine Embroidery, Punch Needle or Applique on knits.

2. Use as a Stabilizer ...

by ironing *Totally Stable* (fusible side down) under or over fabric or design area to be stitched (hoop optional). No need to pin or baste material. For added support on delicate fabrics, use two or more layers.

3. Removal is Easy ...

once stitching is completed, gently peel up and tear away the excess *Totally Stable* to prevent pulling, tearing or distorting of stitches. The fabric underneath is completely free of sticky or unsightly residue.

Try Sulky Totally Stable on the convenient 8" personal roll for quick use, with minimal wastage, when doing computerized machine embroidery. Also available in 1 yard packages and by yardage on a bolt.

*Test for proper heat setting before using on projects made of Nylon or other fabrics that could begin to melt when ironed.

Quick Reference
Totally Stable
Step-by-Step Projects found in the Concepts in Sulky Book Series

"Padded Upside Down Satin Applique" by Peggy Layton, p. 30 *Applique Concepts in Sulky Book 900B3*

"3-D UltraSuede Chicadee Applique" by Peggy Oberbeck, p. 16 & 17, *Applique Concepts in Sulky Book 900B3*

"3-D UltraSuede Parrot Applique" by Peggy Oberbeck, p. 14 & 15 *Applique Concepts in Sulky Book 900B3*

"Charted Needle-work by Machine" by Joyce Drexler, p. 6, 15 & 16, *Concepts in Sulky Book 900B1*

"Special Effects Ultra Suede Applique Lighted, Musical Christmas Tree" by Peggy Oberbeck, p. 26 & 27, *Applique Concepts in Sulky Book 900B3*

21

Quick Reference
Totally Stable
Step-by-Step Projects found in the Concepts in Sulky Book Series

◄ *"Crazy Patchwork Book Cover by Joyce Drexler, p. 9 & 12 Quilting Concepts in Sulky Book 900B7*

"Layered Piecing with Raw Edge Applique" by Virgie Fisher, p. 17-19 Embellishing Concepts in Sulky Book 900B8 ►

"Thread Sketched Quilted Indian" by Cheryl Phillips, p. 13-15 Quilting Concepts in Sulky Book 900B7 ►

◄ *"Appliqueing Natural Fibers" by Joyce Drexler, p. 5-6 Surface Design Concepts in Sulky Book 900B6*

◄ *"Ribbons of Sulky Thread" by Libby Lehman, p. 2-8 Quilting Concepts in Sulky Book 900B7* ►

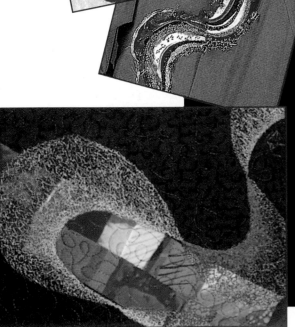

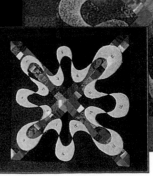

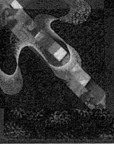

22

Quick Reference
Totally Stable
Step-by-Step Projects found in the Concepts in Sulky Book Series

"Shaded Thread Applique using Totally Stable as a Template"
by Libby Lehman, p. 19-20
Surface Design Concepts in Sulky Book 900B6 ▶

◀ *"Using Totally Stable to make a Southwest Cincher Thread Spray"*
by Kathy Stachowicz, p. 43
Embellishing Concepts in Sulky Book 900B8

"Using Totally Stable as a stitching pattern for Cutwork Windows" ▶
by Joyce Drexler, p. 15
Patchwork Concepts in Sulky Book 900B9

◀ *"Totally Stable Template for making Bias Edging for Reversible Vests & Jackets"*
by Maggie Walker, p. 31
Patchwork Concepts in Sulky Book 900B9

"Resurfacing Ready-mades with Sulky Sliver and Patchwork using Totally Stable to make a pattern" ▶
by Joyce Drexler, p. 46 & 47
Embellishing Concepts in Sulky Book 900B8

23

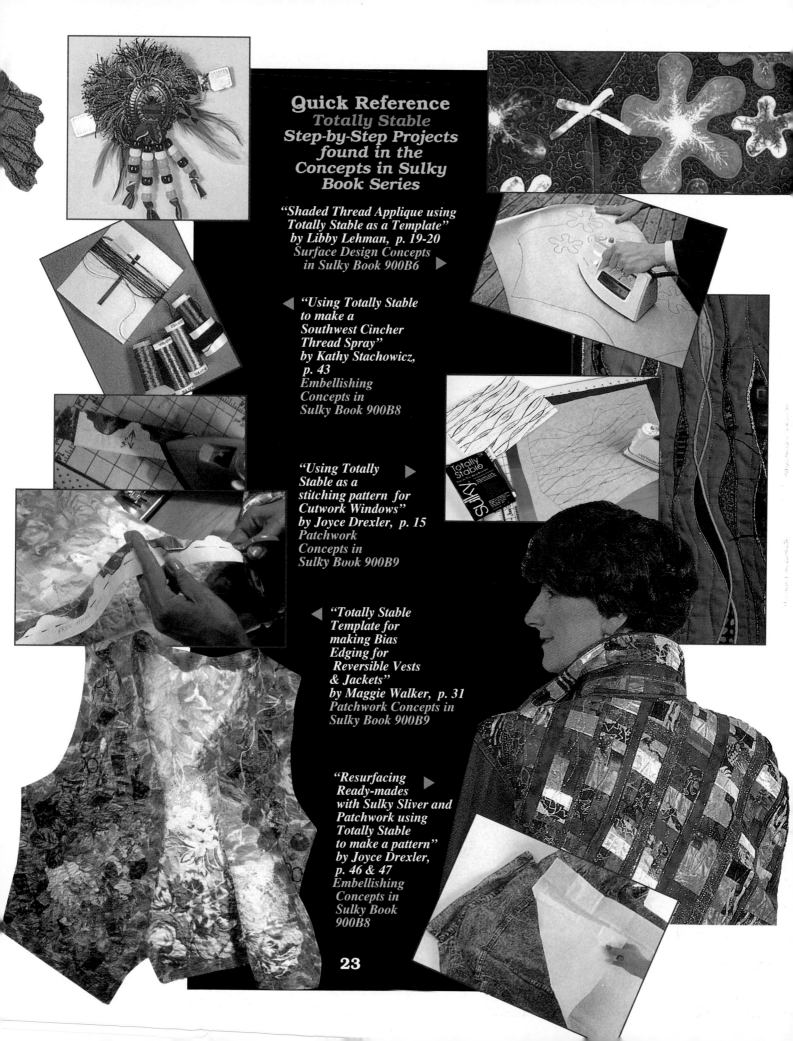

• What? • When? • Where? • Why? & • How? to Sucessfully use ...

Sulky Sticky™

What is Sulky Sticky Stabilizer?

Sticky is a self-adhesive, non-woven, temporary tear-away stabilizer that is super easy to use as a hooping aid and stabilizer which saves time and provides super stability combined with effortless removal, and it doesn't gum up your needle.

When would I use Sticky Self-Adhesive Stabilizer?

You would use Sticky for hooped computerized machine embroidery. It would also be utilized anytime an item that is too small to fit in a hoop needs to be secured in a hoop for any type of stitchery.

Where would I use Sticky Self-Adhesive Stabilizer?

Use Sticky to secure hard-to-hoop small items for computerized machine embroidery and monogramming, i.e. pockets, edges, button rows, ribbons, cuffs, collars, socks, neckties, linen, silk handkerchiefs, doll clothes, etc., as well as for counted cross stitch, silk ribbon work, and hand embroidery in a hoop. It is also ideal for protecting edges of needlepoint and cross stitch canvas by folding a strip of Sticky over them. Use Sticky to secure hats in the Hoop-it-All™ Frame when embroidering.

Be sure to check out the projects featured in this book starting on page 100.

Why would I use Sulky Sticky Self-Adhesive Stabilizer instead of another kind of Sulky Stabilizer?

It is ideal for "hoopless embroidery" because it eliminates hoop marks when embroidering on all fabrics including sweatshirt fleece, UltraSuede, velvet, brushed velour, brushed denim, silk, flannel, nylon, knitted fabrics and caps. Items adhered to Sticky stay put during stitching, eliminating registration problems, especially on knits.

How would I use Sulky Sticky Self-Adhesive Stabilizer?

• *Hoop Sulky Sticky with the release paper side up, the way you would hoop a piece of fabric. Using a small knife or straight pin, score the paper and pull it away from the adhesive layer. Finger press your fabric to the Sticky. Attach the hoop to the embroidery machine. If more support is needed for flimsy or unstable fabrics, spray Sulky KK 2000 on a layer or two of Sulky Tear-Easy or Sulky Stiffy Stabilizer and slip it under the hoop; embroider. For best results, remove excess Sticky from fabric within several hours of application.*

• *For "Hoopless" Embroidery use only the outer portion of the hoop for your embroidery machine. Peel off and discard the paper release sheet from the Sticky and affix the adhesive side to the bottom of the outer portion of your hoop. Place your fabric on the hoop and finger press to adhere it to the Sticky. Put the hoop on your embroidery machine. If more support is needed, place a layer or two of Sulky Tear-Easy or Stiffy Stabilizer under the hoop, and embroider. To remove any adhesive buildup on the hoop, use Goo-Gone™, which is available at most fabric and hardware stores.*

• *For hand work projects like counted cross stitch, silk ribbon embroidery, etc. when the fabric isn't large enough to fit in the hoop, affix Sulky Sticky to outer edges of fabric to make them larger.*

A Quick Guide to Using Sulky Sticky™ for Computerized Machine Embroidery.

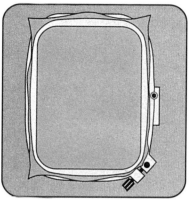

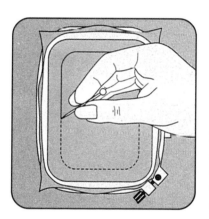

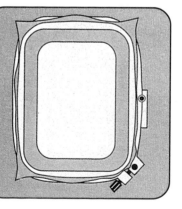

1. Hoop Sulky Sticky with the release paper side up, the way you would hoop a piece of fabric for machine embroidery.

Option #2 -
Or remove the paper release sheet and adhere the Sticky to the back of the larger hoop. Either insert the inner hoop for more stability while embroidering or leave it off.

2. Score the paper *release side with a small knife like an Exacto™ Knife or a straight pin.*

3. Peel off the paper release sheet. Self-adhesive, non-woven Sticky is now exposed and ready for the garment or piece to be affixed for embroidery by machine.

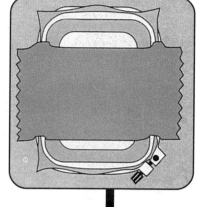

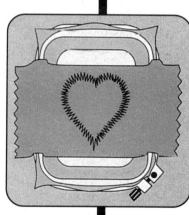

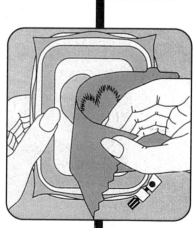

4. Place the garment or piece to be embroidered over the hoop; position as desired with the grain line of the fabric straight. Finger press to smooth in place. Fabric can be removed and repositioned several times before Sticky will no longer hold.

5. Attach the embroidery hoop to the machine and embroider according to the machine manufacturer's instructions.

Note: When using Sticky, the inside ring of the hoop is usually not used over the fabric.

6. After embroidery is completed, gently pull away the fabric from the Sticky. When the embroidery is completed, you can actually "patch" the Sticky in the area that was removed with a scrap piece of Sticky a little larger than the hole. Place the garment or fabric for the next embroidery without removing the entire piece of Sticky from the hoop. You can continue in this manner until the Sticky no longer holds. At that time, hoop a new piece of Sticky as in #'s 1 through 5. Always remove excess Sticky before applying heat from an iron or clothes dryer. For best results, remove excess Sticky from fabric within several hours of application.

Fran D. McAvity
Sulky International
Canada

Fran was born in Saint John, New Brunswick, Canada and raised in Vancouver, British Columbia. Her original profession was as a Medical Technologist with a Masters in Chemistry. She previously worked in a General Hospital as a Thyroid Researcher, in private laboratories and in a Children's Hospital in the Intensive Care Nursery.

In 1983 she started an industrial embroidery company called, "Wind Tinged" which did custom embroidery, machine sales, original design digitizing, and embroidery supply sales. In 1985 she started the Canadian branch for the German Company that makes most Sulky products. She presently supervises the operation of two of their embroidery supply warehouses in Vancouver and Toronto. She was involved in the sales and training for digitizing systems as well. Fran has written for Stitches Magazine and lectured at the Imprinted Sportswear Show in Toronto.

How to think like a professional embroiderer so you can use the right embroidery supplies to obtain picture-perfect computerized machine embroidery.

by Fran D. McAvity and Joyce Drexler

In order to effectively use embroidery supplies, you need to have a better understanding of the variables within your designs and how they affect the fabrics onto which they are applied. This means understanding more about the construction of the design and how each stitch or group of stitches affects the fabrics when they are applied. Because the embroidery process contains many variables, **"A WHEEL"** may help you to follow these variables as changes occur in design parameters, fabrics, and thread mediums.

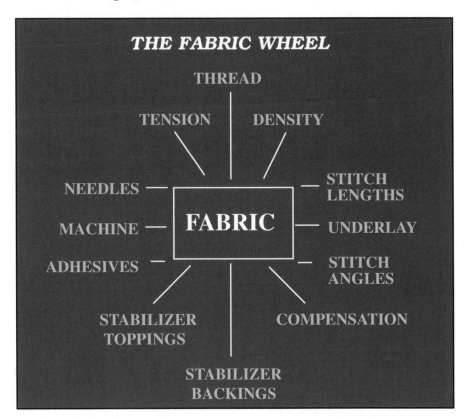

The **thread** is the main embroidery ingredient, with the **backings, toppings, and adhesives** acting as embroidery "aids". The **machine, needles, and tensions** are our tools, and our skill with these tools determine the end result. All of the above items are our choices. The stitch length, density, underlay, stitch directions and compensation are the components of our embroidery design. The machine will only stitch what it is programmed to do by you.

Some rules of thumb:
- Try one new thing at a time
- Test before you run an actual project
- Imagine doing the job by hand
- Use common sense

Let's take the FABRIC WHEEL and make pyramids of information from each spoke.

What is an Embroidery Design?

It is important to know what makes up an embroidery design so you can determine where it is appropriate to use that design and on what fabrics.

Stitch Types within the Design.

Designs may be constructed from 3 basic stitch types ...

1. The "Running" Stitch, also known as the "Walking Stitch", has only one parameter ... the stitch length. It can be created manually one at a time (like joining the dots) or as a run from point "a" to point "b" where the line from "a" to "b" is divided equally by a predetermined stitch length.

2. The "Satin" Stitch, also known as a "Column Stitch", is a zig-zag that is closed up very tightly so that the stitches actually lie beside each other. This stitch has two parameters: the stitch length is now the column width (set with Stitch Width Selector); the stitch density is how far apart the stitches are set from each other (set with Stitch Length Selector).

3. The "Fill" Stitch, also known as the "Stepp Stitch", is normally used when the width of a column is too wide for a satin stitch to sew properly; it is simply multiple rows of running stitches which can only sew in one up or down direction. It is governed by three parameters: a predetermined stitch length; the density (how far apart the rows of stitches are from each other), and the offset which determines the pattern of the fill. If the offset was determined at 100% (or 0), each needle penetration from every row would be sewn directly under one another... creating a column-like effect. If the offset is determined at 33% (normal), the needle penetrations are staggered evenly between the rows, returning to the original "set" at every third row, creating a blended look. Many creative effects can be produced by changing the configurations of the offsets.

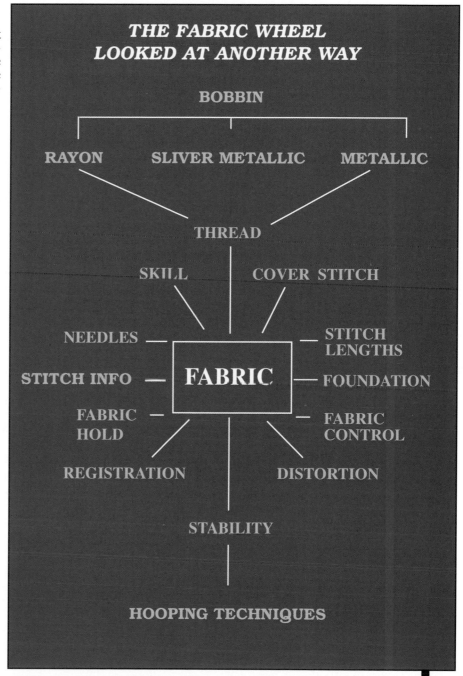

THE FABRIC WHEEL LOOKED AT ANOTHER WAY

BOBBIN

RAYON   SLIVER METALLIC   METALLIC

THREAD

SKILL   COVER STITCH

NEEDLES   STITCH LENGTHS

STITCH INFO   **FABRIC**   FOUNDATION

FABRIC HOLD   FABRIC CONTROL

REGISTRATION   DISTORTION

STABILITY

HOOPING TECHNIQUES

Stitch Parameters (Design Components)

DENSITY
Density is the number of Stitches Per Inch.

There is no density to a running stitch as this is just one single line of stitching. Density of a satin (column) stitch or a fill stitch can best be described as a "Cover Stitch". How close together are the threads? How well do they "cover" the fabric?

I like to use the analogy of building a deck onto your house. To achieve a normal density, you would only buy enough boards to "cover" the area of the deck. An open density would mean that you have left some space between the boards, either for looks or for economical benefits. Density is also affected by the thickness of the chosen embroidery thread.

UNDERLAY
The underlay (underlayers) is the "Foundation".

Again, there are no underlays to a running stitch. The satin (column) stitch can have either a running stitch type underlay or a zig-zag (open column) type underlay, or a combination of both. The fill stitch can have open rows of running type stitches, placed at a 90° angle to the cover stitches. This would be similar to the foundation beams or trusses of your deck, giving support to your deck boards. The fabric will dictate the closeness of the underlay rows.

The underlays may also be used double, producing a netting or diamond shaped look. Underlay stitches must always be used at a different angle to the cover stitches to prevent the cover stitches from blending in with the un-

derlays. Underlays have also been used to give height to a column of embroidery. When used as a foundation, underlays are totally fabric dependent. Stretch fabrics (jersey, knits) and fabrics with nap (towels, sweaters, corduroy) or a combination of both (stretch terry) will all require different underlay applications.

STITCH ANGLES
The angle of direction of the stitches provides fabric control.

The most common example of fabric control is the direction of fill stitches on stretch fabrics. Most finished goods stretch left to right. Using running stitches up and down on fabric that stretches left to right only "Opens" the stretch, giving a wavy puckered look to your embroidery. This is not fixable! Stitches on stretch fabrics must always run with the stretch or at a slight angle to the stretch to "set" the stretch. This applies to both underlays and cover stitches. Because of the mechanism of actual stitch creation by your embroidery machine, the direction of the stitches can also provide different looks or effects.

COMPENSATION
Embroidery is really the art of "Distortion".

All fabrics will demonstrate a "pooch and pull" * syndrome. This is where you have to imagine doing this process by hand. As you pull the stitch tight (tension), you exert a "pull". As you sew one row after another, you push the fabric along ahead of you, creating a "pooch".

Don't forget, you are adding more thread to an already made fabric. Examples: When creating a satin or col-

*First described by Walter Floriani, Jr.

umn of stitches, each stitch will pull towards the center of the column and the end of the column will become elongated or pooched. You end up with a long, skinny column. To COMPENSATE for this, make the column wider and shorter, letting the sewing process pull and pooch the column to the correct shape.

When creating a fill stitch, the stitches at the end of the rows will pull back towards the center and the entire area will be pooched in the direction of sewing. The COMPENSATION in this instance is creating a wide, short oval in order to sew a circle of full stitches.

Compensation can be either built into the design or created as a % compensation by computer software. The % compensation gives an "overthrow" to the width of the design segments and, although helpful, is not as accurate as the compensation built into the original design. Design component size and shape will dictate the amount of compensation required. Stretch and nap fabrics can pose additional challenges.

STITCH LENGTHS
The single most abused factor on the Wheel

The stitch length is the only constant component in the embroidery process. Because we are sewing hundreds and thousands of stitches at a glance, we tend to ignore the individual stitch lengths hidden within. Too long a stitch makes for baggy embroidery and stitches that loop and/or get caught, pulling away from the design. Too short a stitch is not a stitch at all and leads to thread breaks and holes. The embroidery process needs to be as smooth as possible. Stitch lengths will be governed by fabrics, by thread size and type, as well as by special fill stitch effects.▼

FABRIC VARIABLES:
1. The yarn size (or thickness) of the fabric itself.
2. The texture of the fabric.
3. The actual weave of the fabric.
4. The stretch factor.
5. Any other notable problem areas.

These are but a few examples of how to type or describe the fabric you will be working with. Make sure that you "feel" your fabrics before embroidering them ... push and pull them around. This will help you avoid unnecessary stitch removal. Create some categories of your own. You are now on your way to making recipes, or putting designs to fabric.

FABRIC CATEGORIES

Examples	Yarn Size	Texture	Weave	Stretch	Other
DENIM	heavy	smooth	tight	not normally	
NYLON	fine	smooth	tight	no	slippery
TERRY	medium	lumpy	loose	no	
CORDUROY	heavy	varying	tight	no	
KNITS	varies	varies	varies	yes	
LEATHER		smooth		no	leaves holes
LYCRA/ SPANDEX & SILK	fine	smooth	tight	yes	

IT IS SO IMPORTANT TO BE CONSTANTLY AWARE OF STITCH LENGTHS AS THIS SINGLE FACTOR IS THE UNDERLYING CAUSE OF MOST EMBROIDERERS' HEARTACHES.

APPLYING STITCH PARAMETERS TO FABRICS

There is a "perfect" design for every fabric situation. In the beginning, designs were created stitch by stitch. Today, we rely on sophisticated software to produce our designs. It is still, however, important to at least understand what has been produced by computer so that we can apply design component knowledge to fabrics. *P.S. It's not rocket science...it's more like doing puzzles!*

Note that the fabric is placed in the middle of the WHEEL. Design parameters will change depending on the fabric. Let's look at the fabric variables that will affect the embroidery design.

Fabrics only become difficult to embroider for two reasons: if you don't see each project as an individual, unique procedure, and if you don't consider all of the properties of the fabric before beginning. If you want to put the same design onto denim and knit shirts, what decisions do you have to make? Do I need underlay ... is the stitch direction suitable for stretch ... how much compensation do I need ... can I get away with the same design parameters on both types of fabric? Always choose a design that will run on the most difficult fabric well. Professional embroiderers sometimes have to stitch hundreds of these designs, so they may have to look at what is the most efficient one for each individual fabric and have more than one version of the design. If you are doing several applications of the same design on varying fabrics, then you may have to rely on embroidery aids to help smooth the difference. So let's look at our tools.

THREADS:

The Embroidery Thread is your "Art Medium" - like painting with thread. This is not a 2 dimensional art form but it is actually 3-D or 4-D if you add colors!

Thread comes in different sizes and make-ups. The most popular decorative thread is Sulky 40 wt. & 30 wt. Rayon because of its high quality, natural luster, and wonderful "sewability". Other popular threads include Sulky Original Metallic and Sulky Sliver Metallic. All Sulky thread spools have smooth "snap-ends" on both ends to eliminate the "nasty gash" found on other brands which can cause the thread to tangle and snag as it is delivered to the needle. The "snap-ends" open and close easily to free the thread end or hold it securely for storage. Most are cross-wound to ensure smooth thread flow and consistently superior stitch quality. Use either a matching 40 wt. Rayon Thread, Sulky Bobbin Thread or Sulky Polyester Invisible Thread in the bobbin when machine embroidering.

> *All Sulky Decorative Threads are an especially exciting art medium which have special characteristics. We don't need to know why we like them as much as we need to know their pet peeves! Rayon hates chemical washes and bleach. Metallic Threads hate abrasion and short stitches because metallics simply don't bend well into small stitches; machine burrs, stiff or rough fabrics or stabilizers can "break" the metal wrap, causing the metal to unravel at the needle. The most common mistakes when using Metallic Threads are using too small a needle size, too short a stitch, and sewing too fast.*

Sulky 40 wt. Rayon: The most commonly used weight because they are: • Available in 231 colors including multi-colored and variegated shades. • The correct weight for which most programmed embroidery designs have been digitized. • Manufactured in Germany using the highest grade of raw goods for smooth delivery. • Color fast. • Completely washable (avoid chlorine bleach or other optical brighteners) with a shine that lasts through laundering. • Usable in the bobbin when both sides will be visible. • And, they have a longer life, do not fray and fuzz in the machine, and do not shrink like cotton thread. Use a needle size 11/75 or 12/80.

Sulky 30 wt. Rayon: Available in 102 solid colors, they are 1/3 thicker and heavier than Sulky 40 wt., but with similar qualities. When designs are enlarged from their original digitized state, 30 wt. Rayon will fill the design better than 40 wt. Some embroiderers prefer it when using Sulky Puffy Foam™ for 3-D Embroidery or for fill or cover stitches when embroidering with a light color thread on a dark fabric, or vice-versa. Use a size 14/90 needle. Not suitable for fine detail work.

Sulky Original Metallic Thread: Available in 36 solid and multi-colors that are made by wrapping the finest metallic foil around a strong polyester core, in most colors, to create a top quality thread that works very well and is easy to thread in your embroidery machine needle. (Size 14/90 Embroidery, Metallic, or Top Stitching Needle recommended because of its large eye, deep groove and slightly rounded point to prevent fraying at the needle.) It is completely washable in cool or warm water; avoid chlorine bleach or other optical brighteners. Iron on low temperature. In the bobbin, use either a matching color Sulky Metallic, 40 wt. Rayon or Sulky Bobbin or Polyester Invisible Thread. Reduce the top tension.

Sulky Sliver™ Metallic Thread: Available in 24 brilliant solid and multi-colors whose ultimate sparkle is unsurpassed. Sulky Sliver is a thin, flat, ribbon-like polyester film that is metalized with aluminum to make it brilliantly reflective. Machine washable, dry at a low heat setting; cover with a press cloth to iron. For best results on a sewing machine, use on a vertical spool pin which allows the spool to turn while stitching. Reduce the top tension. Use a size 14/90 Embroidery or Metallic Needle. In the bobbin, use either a matching color Sulky original Metallic, 40 wt. Rayon, Sulky Bobbin or Polyester Invisible Thread.

TIPS FOR EMBROIDERING WITH METALLIC THREAD:

• Keep metallic thread covered until you use it. Dry or dirty thread breaks.
• Make sure the design was digitized for metallic thread.
• Don't use metallic thread for small lettering.
• Keep your tensions loose. The bobbin in the bobbin case (removable type) should just support itself when held by the thread.
• The bobbin thread should be the thinnest possible.
• Use a new needle with a large eye.
• The material should be as soft as possible without being too fine or delicate. Hard or stiff material is abrasive to metallic thread.
• The backing stabilizer should also be soft and pliable.
• All parts of the machine should be smooth and in excellent working order. Any little flaws or rough areas will break the metallic foil, causing it to fray.
• Reduce the speed of the machine.

TEMPORARY SPRAY ADHESIVES:
HOLD two pieces of FABRIC together as well as making all stabilizers (except Heat-Away) an adhesive.

Sulky KK 2000 Temporary Spray Adhesive was developed for applique, but it also helps provide drum-tight hooping for stretch fabrics when sprayed onto the backing, allowing these fabrics to be placed in their own natural lie. This is particularly useful when dealing with large hoop areas. KK 2000 also helps stop warping of knit rows during embroidery, and it is great for "unhoopables" such as collars cut on the bias, pocket flaps, etc. as well as for mending holes by spraying the damaged area together along with a suitable backing. An alternative to using adhesives is to use iron-on Sulky Totally Stable or self-adhesive Sulky Sticky. Note: Not all spray adhesives are alike. **Sulky KK 2000** has been formulated with highly concentrated material and a heavier-than-air gas propellant which makes it **the only safe, non-toxic, non-flammable, ozone-friendly temporary adhesive on the market today.** It has an excellent spray nozzle with good directional flow to eliminate wasteful, harmful over-spraying. It is a temporary glue which does not make fabric permanently stiff as others can. KK 2000 completely absorbs into the fibers of the fabric within 24-36 hours; it will disappear completely after about 2 to 5 days, while other spray adhesives remain stiff and fused with white residue many months after application. One short spray with KK 2000 is sufficient, while butane-propelled adhesives need 2 or more cloud-producing sprays. Always spray away from the machine or machine parts ... machines hate glue!

> *Note: Not all spray adhesives are alike.* **Sulky KK 2000** *has been formulated with highly concentrated material and a heavier-than-air gas propellant which makes it* **the only safe, non-toxic, non-flammable, ozone-friendly, temporary spray adhesive on the market today.** *It has an excellent spray nozzle with good directional flow to eliminate wasteful, harmful over-spraying.*

HOME EMBROIDERY MACHINES:
Stand-alone machines, or sewing machines that have the added features of built-in, professional-style embroidery; a separate embroidery unit; and/or have digitizing possibilities through lap-top or conventional computers. The machine is responsible for STITCH FORMATION.

You need to know your machine well. What are its limitations in sewing area, minimum-maximum stitch lengths, variable speed and tension requirements? Do you understand the thread paths, tension assemblies and hook assemblies? Make sure that timely maintenance is always performed.

NEEDLES:
Make a hole large enough to pass the thread through without breakage.

NEEDLES COME IN A VARIETY OF TYPES AND SIZES:

BALL POINT - Glides between the fibers of knits.
SHARP - Cuts its way through heavy, tightly woven fabrics.
UNIVERSAL - Works well on both lighter wovens and knits.
WEDGE - "Pops" or punches a hole (leather).

A dull or damaged needle can cause puckering and flagging. Change needles often.

When doing embroidery with a single strand of Sulky 40 wt. Rayon Thread, depending on the weight of fabric, use the smallest size of either an Embroidery, Top Stitch or Denim Needle 75/11, 80/12, 90/14 that is large enough to accommodate the thread, while penetrating the fabric without breaking, but making the smallest hole. When using Sulky 30 wt., or more than one thread through the needle, use a size larger needle. Use a Metallic style needle for Metallic Threads.

STABILIZER TOPPINGS:
TO ENSURE STITCH REGISTRATION

It is important that stitches "go where they are put". Toppings stop stitches from being dragged (shortened) through loose fabric weaves, distorted in stretch weaves, and from getting "lost" inside uneven fabrics like toweling and corduroy. Sulky Solvy and Super Solvy (water soluble) and Sulky Heat-Away (heat disintegrating) are most commonly used because when you remove them, there is no unsightly residue left behind. In some cases, Sulky Tear-Easy would be the best choice when you can stop stitching before the design is completed, tear away the Tear-Easy, then cover the outer edges of the design while completing the stitching.

The embroidery process requires that the fabric be placed into a movable hoop system under a stationary sewing machine head. In order for the stitches to "register" or be placed exactly where the design dictates, the fabric needs to be fairly rigid in the hoop. The expression is known as "drum-tight" hooping. Do not confuse this expression with "stretched tight" as this practice is the common cause of puckering and holes. FABRICS SHOULD ALWAYS BE SEWN IN THEIR OWN NATURAL LIE. Our first line of stabilization is backings or "stabilizers". **Sulky Stabilizers,** except for Heat-Away, **are all non-woven so they don't stretch in any direction.** Some tear away: Tear-Easy, Stiffy; some wash away: Solvy and Super Solvy; some disintegrate with heat: Heat-Away; some cut away: Cut-Away Plus and Cut-Away Soft 'n Sheer; some iron-on: Totally Stable; or are self-adhesive: Sticky.

Once you have chosen a design and fabric, the next part of the recipe is choosing a suitable stabilizer backing. If fabric stability is required only during the stitching process, a tear-away stabilizer backing is suitable. If stability is needed after fabrics have been washed to control shrinkage and prevent sagging of the embroidery, then a cut-away backing may be indicated. **Weight of the backing depends entirely on the design and fabric makeup.** There are varied theories on how many layers of a backing should be used. I recommend not more than 2. Most professionals never hoop two pieces of stabilizer; they spray the second piece with Sulky KK 2000 and slide it under the hoop.

The end use of the article is important. A soft and pliable backing like Sulky Soft 'n Sheer can be desirable in garments worn next to the skin. It is best to have some of all types on hand. Two top factors to keep in mind when selecting a stabilizer backing are, a design's stitch count and the type of garment or fabric to be embroidered. It doesn't matter what worked best on your last project or someone else's project, if the design's stitch count and/or fabric are different, you have to experiment to find out what will work best with this combination.

TENSION:
BALANCE of top thread and bobbin thread.

Every thread (brand, weight, or type) has a specific tensile strength. Operator SKILL must be developed to set the pressure or amount of pull between top and bottom threads as light as possible, and to find the correct balance between top thread and bobbin thread. Overly tight tension can cause puckering; too loose top tension or too tight bobbin tension can cause a build-up of stitches on the underside. Loops on the surface indicate more tension on top than on the bobbin. The balance can be tested by stitching a 1" high column (example: the letter I). As seen from the back, the bobbin thread will show 1/3 of the width of the column, and the top thread will show 1/3 and 1/3 on each side. Tension begins in the bobbin case. Only for free-motion embroidery work will you have to manually adjust the top tension, as most home-style computerized sewing/embroidery machines self-adjust the tension for you.

BUILDING RECIPES:
First pick a fabric, then an appropriate design. Use the "WHEEL" to set scenarios as to choice of machine, thread, needle, tension. Plan which embroidery aids you can use to help overcome design to fabric problems.

Keep a notebook! Where do you make your most common mistakes putting a design onto fabric and why:

A. Using predesigned keyboard lettering ... think about font styles, lock stitches, sizes.

B. Using stock designs...can you figure out the construction?

C. Using "original" designs ... either home made or made to order.

You'll find lots of recipes to try! Embroidery is a bit like cooking ... so don't worry if you haven't got all the exact ingredients. Try some new variations!

"Happy puzzles and here's to great embroidery!" --- Fran

Computerized Machine Embroidery Tips
by Malah Peterson
Professional Embroiderer
Another professional opinion

1. Hooping the Fabric: The most important aspect of machine embroidery besides the backing is hooping the fabric properly. The fabric must be in the hoop taut, but in its natural lay, not stretched out of shape. Tighten the hoop screw so the fabric won't slip while embroidering. When possible, test on scraps of fabric before putting the design on the actual garment. You may need to add an extra backing on fabrics that tend to pucker --- *Satin is the worst!*

2. On Woven Fabric, I use tear-aways like Tear-Easy, Stiffy and Totally Stable. *The thinner the fabric, the heavier the stabilizer; the heavier the fabric, the thinner the stabilizer.*

3. On Knit Fabric, it's just the opposite as wovens. I use lightweight Cut-Away Soft 'n Sheer on lighter weight knits, and heavier Cut-Away Plus on heavier knits. (This is as a general rule --- there may be exceptions.) If I am stitching on something that stretches, like leather, or is hard to hoop because of its unusual shape or small size, I use Sulky Sticky or spray another stabilizer with Sulky KK-2000 Temporary Spray Adhesive. When stitching small lettering, I always use Solvy on top of fabric that has a nap and is washable, like terry cloth, velour, polar fleece and pique shirts; on fabrics that are not washable, I use Heat-Away.

4. Lined Satin Jackets: Which stabilizer I use on these jackets depends on the lining. If there is a quilted or heavy lining, I use lighter Tear-Easy. If there is a thin lining, I use a heavier Stiffy tear-away <u>in</u> the hoop and then I slide under the hoop as many layers of Sulky Tear-Easy as I need to keep the satin from puckering. But the wider the width of the satin stitch used, the more puckering

---

"The general rule I use for backing is to use a tear-away stabilizer on woven fabrics and a cut-away on knits or stretch fabrics." --- Malah

---

you will get, and some may not be avoidable unless you reduce the width.

The same is true of windbreakers which may have a puckered texture in the fabric. If there is a mesh lining, I am sure to use a sharp needle to pierce the mesh. Otherwise, the needle tends to glance off the lining and go through the holes of the mesh.

5. Needles: I use the appropriate type and size needle for the fabric type.

Always do a test.

A Beginner's Guide to Successful SULKY® STABILIZING for Computerized Machine Embroidery

This chart contains basic guidelines for your use in building recipes as you take into consideration all of the spokes of the wheel from pages 26 - 34. Make any Stabilizer (except Heat-Away) a "Sticky-type" by spraying it with Sulky KK 2000™ Temporary Spray Adhesive.
* Indicates in the hoop. ** Indicates under the hoop. Use a new needle in size indicated.
Always hoop fabric in its relaxed lie --- do not distort the weave or grain when hooping!

Fabric	Needle Size (U)Universal (B) Ballpoint (S) Sharp	Backing	Topping
Canvas	Denim 16/100 (S)	Tear-Easy or Stiffy	N/A
Cotton Sheeting	12/80 14/90 (S/U)	Soft'n Sheer, Stiffy, or Totally Stable	N/A
Corduroy	12/80 14/90 (S/U)	Tear-Easy or Totally Stable	* Heat-Away
Denim/Shirt (Med. wt.)	12/80 14/90 (S/U)	Stiffy or 2 layers of Tear-Easy	N/A
Dress Shirt	12/80 14/90 (U)	Stiffy or 2 layers of Tear-Easy	N/A
Golf Shirt/Pique	11/75 12/80 (U/B)	* Soft'n Sheer or Cut-Away Plus with ** Stiffy	* S.Solvy
Golf Shirt/Knit	11/75 12/80 (U/B)		* S.Solvy
Hats	12/80 14/90 (U)	Sticky	* S.Solvy
Soft Leather	Leather Needle	Sticky or Tear-Easy	N/A
Lingerie/Silk	11/75 (U/B)	*2 layers of Tear-Easy with ** one 1 layer of Tear-Easy	N/A
Lycra	11/75 (U/B)	Cut-Away Plus or Stiffy	N/A
Nylon Windbreaker	11/75 (U/B)	*2 layers of Tear-Easy with ** one 1 layer of Tear-Easy	N/A
Quilted Fabric	12/80 (U)	Tear-Easy	N/A
Lined Satin Jacket *Quilted*	11/75 12/80 (U/B)	Tear-Easy	N/A
Unlined Satin Jacket *Light*	11/75 12/80 (U/B)	* Stiffy with **2-3 layers Tear-Easy	N/A
Sweater Knit	12/80 14/90 (B)	* Cut-Away Plus with ** Stiffy	* S.Solvy
Sweatshirt Knit	12/80 14/90 (B)	* Cut-Away Plus with ** Stiffy	* S.Solvy
T-Shirt Knit	11/75 12/80 (U/B)	* Soft'n Sheer or Cut-Away Plus with ** Stiffy	* S.Solvy
Terry Cloth	12/80 14/90 (U/B)	Stiffy or 2 layers of Tear-Easy	*Heat-Away
Ultra Suede	12/80 14/90 (U/B)	Sticky or Stiffy	N/A
Velvet/Velveteen	12/80 (B)	Sticky or 2 layers of Tear-Easy	*Heat-Away
Vinyl	12/80 (U)	Sticky or Tear-Easy	N/A

• What? • When? • Where? • Why? & • How? to Sucessfully use ...

Sulky Puffy Foam™

What is Puffy Foam?

Puffy Foam is a high quality Ethylene Vinyl Acetate Film that is made specifically for use on home sewing machines to add flair, 3-dimension and excitement to your designs. It is non-toxic, water-resistant and machine washable (machine dry on low) but it is flammable and cannot be dry-cleaned. It comes in 12 colors in each of two thicknesses, 2 mm and 3 mm, to create different stitching effects, and there is virtually no waste because even very small pieces can be used. Layers can be stacked to make 4mm and 5mm thicknesses... or whatever will fit under your presser foot or darning foot.

When would I use Puffy Foam?

Whenever you want to add wonderful new Dimension to Computerized Embroidery, Machine Satin Stitches and/or Free-Motion Satin Stitching.

Where would I use Puffy Foam?

Use it on computerized embroidery designs that are especially digitized for Puffy Foam or that have satin-stitch elements in the pattern. It's fantastic with tapered elegant-style lettering. It's fun to use with your satin or column-like decorative stitches. Use under the satin stitch when you applique.

Be sure to check out the projects featured in this book starting on page 36.

Why would I use Puffy Foam instead of other foam?

Puffy Foam perforates cleaner, allowing it to tear away more easily because it was specifically made to be used on home sewing machines for embroidery, applique and decorative satin stitches.

How would I use Puffy Foam?

• *Puffy Foam works best on designs that feature either a satin stitch edge or underlay techniques that will perforate the foam prior to stitching the top layer. Not all machines and/or design cards are appropriate for both weights of Puffy Foam. Do a test sample before applying to finished project.*

• *Puffy Foam makes the stitching stand well above the fabric. Use one of the 12 Puffy Foam colors that is closest to your thread color to make the foam less noticeable if any shows through your stitching.*

• *It is being widely seen commercially in headgear and washable wearables. Look for special computerized embroidery cards made especially for Puffy Foam at your favorite sewing store.*

• *Cut a piece of Puffy Foam slightly larger than the design area that you want to "puff"; place it on top of the fabric that is being embroidered, appliqued or satin stitched so the foam is between the fabric and the thread being applied.*

• *To embroider over Puffy Foam, hoop the receiving fabric along with the appropriate stabilizer backing. Place the Puffy Foam on top of the area to be puffed, and hold it in place while you take the first few stitches; or spray Sulky KK 2000 Temporary Spray Adhesive on the foam and finger press to adhere it in place.*

• *Try cutting 1/4" strips of Puffy Foam and feeding them through a large cording, piping or beading foot, treating them like any cord that you would satin stitch over.*

• *Save all of the pieces of Puffy Foam that you tear away once the stitching is completed. You can stitch over even the tiniest piece (example: animal eyes, noses, paws, etc.).*

• *You may want to stitch over the edges again once Puffy Foam is removed. When Puffy Foam has been torn away from the design, if any little "pokies" remain, shrink them with a hair dryer, or place a steam iron very close to them and shoot with steam.*

• *When editing computerized designs to stitch on Puffy Foam, eliminate any straight stitching that goes down the center of a column of satin stitching; simply move it to the edge to help perforate the foam.*

PUFFY FOAM™

General Information

*When using Sulky Puffy Foam, follow a few simple guidelines
and do a test sample before applying to finished project.*

- Puffed designs generally work best on stable fabrics. Hoop your fabric **along with** the appropriate Sulky Stabilizer for that fabric.
- Relax tensions so you don't compress the foam.
- Use the needle type best suited to your base fabric. All needle types will suitably perforate Puffy Foam.
- Carefully choose the design elements that will be puffed. Puffy Foam makes a good accent or focal point, and it looks great mixed with conventional embroidery; wide outlines look terrific over Puffy Foam.
- Choose a color of Puffy Foam that best matches thread color. This allows less density or special editing to be used and, if the thread should separate, it won't be noticeable.
- Vary or combine thicknesses or layers of foam for different effects. Life-like dimension can be added to designs like flowers, tree trunks, balls (basketball, soccer, football, tennis, etc.) by doing the outer third with no Foam, the next third with 1 layer of Foam and the center third with a thicker or double layer of foam.
- Save all scraps for use on small design areas.
- Puff only the satin stitch areas of a design, the wider the satin stitch the better. Fill and ceeding stitches aren't suitable because they compress the foam.
- Cut a piece of Puffy Foam larger than the area to be embroidered.
- Place Foam on top of the hooped fabric and lightly hold it in place while stitching a few stitches to tack it to the fabric. Sulky KK 2000 Temporary Spray Adhesive can also be used.
- After the entire foamed area has been sewn, remove the hoop from the machine and carefully tear away the excess foam.
- Try to use designs where the satin column goes to a tapered end, otherwise you will have to cut away the foam rather than perforating and tearing it.

Working with Keyboard Lettering and Puffy Foam

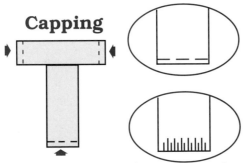

- Use a font style that has wide columns, or widen them using your column width function.
- Outline font styles can work well because they are fully enclosed, with no open ends on columns. (See illustration below).
- Increase density 40% to 60% above normal settings.
- Only satin columns will puff. Fill and Ceeding stitches are not suitable.
- To eliminate gaps, you may need to edit certain letters to overlap more where the sections join.

Capping

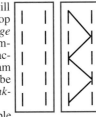

- Arrows point to open column ends where there are no stitches to cut the Foam. If left unedited, Foam will extend from these open ends and it will have to be removed by hand.
- You can *"Cap"* the end of a wide satin stitch column by either placing a satin stitch in the opposite direction, adding running stitches inside the open column, or throwing varying stitch lengths toward the center of the column along the inside column edge while keeping the outside edge straight to cut the Foam and cap the end. Tapering the end is another option.

Digitizing for Foam

- Use underlay techniques that will perforate the Foam prior to the top layer of stitching; a double *"edge walk"* of running stitches combined with a light zig-zag will accomplish this, and tack the foam in place. This technique can be used in combination with *Planking and Capping*.
- Simplify shapes where possible to keep elements more rounded, rather than sharp, and keep the columns as wide as possible. Add more density to any part of the design that will have more than one 2mm layer of foam on it.

Planking

- Try *"Planking"* in areas where columns intersect which can result in collapse of the Foam. Vary stitch length so you don't create a cut line for the Foam.

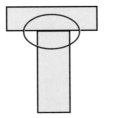

*Care: Machine Washable. Flammable.
Avoid overdrying in a Hot Dryer. Do not Iron or Dry Clean.*

3-D Embroidered & Appliqued Shirt

A Sulky Puffy Foam™ and Sulky Stabilizer Project

As presented by Joyce Drexler on the PBS TV Program "Sew Creative" with Donna Wilder

This design incorporates three different techniques: Satin Stitching over Puffy Foam, Computerized Embroidery and Blanket Stitch Applique. If your machine does not have Embroidery capabilities, I recommend substituting the appliqued Chickadee (reduced) from the Sulky Applique Book 900B-3.

You will need:

✔ **Stabilizers:**
  1 yd. of Totally Stable™ Iron-on
  1/4 yd. Sticky™ Self-Adhesive
  and 1/2 yd. of Super Solvy™ or Tear-Easy™
✔ **Sulky Puffy Foam™**
  3 - 6" x 9" sheets of 2mm Tan or Black
✔ **Sulky 30 wt. Rayon Thread:**
  For Branch: 1057 Dk. Tawny Tan or Black 1005
  For Bird #11 on back of shirt - I substituted:
    Color #1 White - 1001 - Bright White
    Color #2 Yellow - 1055 - Tawny Tan
    Color #3 Gold - 1126 - Tan
    Color #4 - By Passed - No Branch
    Color #5 Gray - 1057 - Dk. Tawny Tan
    Color #6 Black - 1005 - Black
✔ **Memory Craft 9000**
  Sewing/Embroidery Machine
✔ **Machine Needles:**
  A new Top Stitching or
  Embroidery Size 14/90
✔ **Memory Card #116 Bird Designs, Bird #11**
✔ **Ready-made Denim Shirt with flat back**
✔ **Fat Quarters of a Black, Red and Tan Fabric**
  for Birdhouse Applique - *I used M & M Mumm's the Word Fabrics.*
✔ **Sulky KK 2000 Temporary Spray Adhesive** or
  substitute 1 yd. Dbl. Sided Steam-A-Seam™
  Fusible Web
✔ **Fine-Line, Permanent-Ink Marker**
✔ **Applique and Branch Design found on pull-out**
  pattern sheet in the back of this book.

Instructions:

1. Press 2 layers of Totally Stable onto the wrong side of the shirt over the entire area where any stitching will be done.

2. With a fine-line, permanent-ink marker, trace Branch design onto Super Solvy or Tear-Easy Stabilizer. Lightly spray one side of the Puffy Foam with KK 2000 and hand press traced stabilizer pattern onto it in pieces as indicated on the pattern. Lightly spray the other side of the Puffy Foam to make it stay in place on the shirt while stitching each section of the branch.

3. Set your machine for a close satin stitch (width - 6.0, length 1.5). Place an open-toe applique foot or other channelled foot on the machine. Reduce foot pressure. Satin stitch according to the width indicated on the pattern. As branches taper, reduce your width setting accordingly. You may need to help feed the fabric with the foam under the foot. Pull away the perforated foam once the entire piece is stitched. Repeat stitching at a little wider width to cover the edges of foam that may still be showing.

4. Adhere 2 layers of Sulky Sticky under the embroidery hoop. Secure the hoop in the cloth setter. Position the shirt over the hoop so the bird will rest on the lower branch. Smooth the shirt down onto the Sticky. Embroider using recommended Sulky 30 wt. Thread Colors.

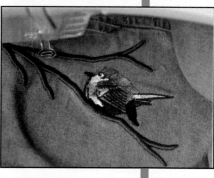

5. Once embroidery is completed, remove the shirt from the hoop and the Sticky. Leave Totally Stable behind the area to be appliqued. Prepare applique pieces by either tracing designs and applying double-sided fusible web, then cutting them out, or by cutting out pieces, then applying KK 2000 Temporary Spray Adhesive to the wrong side of the fabrics. Position on shirt as photo indicates. Blanket stitch by machine using Sulky 30 wt. Rayon Thread. Once all stitching is completed, carefully remove Totally Stable one layer at a time. Repeat techniques using Bird # 11 on the front yoke, if desired.

New Dimensions with Sulky Puffy Foam™

by Pauline Richards

*An edited version from
"SEW NEWS" MAGAZINE
September 1997 issue.*

Elevate machine embroidery to a new level with a very special embroidery foam, a new product that transforms ordinary embroidered motifs into puffy three-dimensional show stoppers.

Made by Debbie Neid

GREAT HEIGHTS

Puff Embroidery is created by satin stitching over thin, flexible Sulky Puffy Foam. The machine needle penetrates the foam as the satin stitches cover and encase a precise shape. This raises the design, completely hiding the base fabric and making the embroidered areas stand out. The foam is perforated in stitching and the excess foam is gently torn away when the design is completed.

Sulky Puffy Foam is available in 2mm and 3mm thicknesses in 12 different colors, with 2mm being the easiest to work with; 2 layers of 2mm can be stacked for a 4mm maximum thickness.

Puffy Foam is made of ethylene vinyl acetate. This flammable material disintegrates when subjected to drycleaning solvents, but is machine washable and dryable, non-toxic and can withstand the heat of a medium-hot iron.

Garments and Home Dec items alike can benefit from the added dimension given by stitching over Puffy Foam.

Note: To order a free Quilt Project Sheet, see Sources p. 137

PERFECT PUFFING POINTERS

❏ While thick foam raises a design more than thin foam, it also increases the possibility of thread and needle breakage and usually necessitates the use of 30 wt. thread for proper coverage.

Thicker foam also will stiffen the base fabric more than 2mm foam and requires the stability of a heavy fabric like denim, or a permanent cut-away stabilizer under a lighter weight fabric.

❏ Use an 80/12 embroidery or ballpoint needle. Although an embroidery needle is ideal when using rayon thread, a ballpoint needle will perforate the foam more completely, so experiment with both.

❏ Thread and foam colors should be of the same color family. Fewer stitches can be used to cover the foam without it showing through.

❏ Choose a simple design with mostly satin stitching --- logos, shapes, symbols or lettering arc ideal. A "fill" area can be stitched with Puffy Foam underneath, but the fill stitch will compress the foam and you will not have as raised an effect as you might have desired when the excess foam is removed.

❏ Because Puffy Foam naturally adds stiffness to an embroidery design area, select the placement carefully.

❏ Puffy Foam usually isn't recommended for use on lightweight fabrics; however, it can be used on the yoke or neckline on form fitting garments.

❏ Prevent fabric distortion or stretch on medium weight fabrics by applying "Sulky Sticky" Stabilizer to the wrong side of the fabric, or if you desire a more permanent stabilization, apply a lightweight fusible tricot interfacing or non-woven Sulky Cut-Away Soft 'n Sheer before embroidering.

Compare the design at right without Puffy Foam to the design below with Puffy Foam.

❏ When a design has both fill and satin stitched areas, stitch the fill parts as normal, stop the machine and insert the Puffy Foam just before stitching the satin stitches.

❏ Achieve the most pleasing results by puffing design segments rather than the entire design. Placing Puffy Foam in closely spaced design areas will create a three-dimensional look.

❏ Remove the excess foam from each completed puffed area before straight stitching or sewing another color puffed area. For example, in the photo to the right, the flower center was stitched without foam. *Note: Straight stitches aren't recommended for use to tear away the foam, and unsightly thread loops will remain rather than consistent flat, straight stitches.*

❏ When puffing a design where satin stitching columns end as a wide satin stitch, such as the design on the featured jacket sleeve, the foam must be cut instead of torn away from the stitching because there isn't stitching at the column end to perforate the foam.

❏ If any foam remains on the outside of the thread, use a hair dryer to "shrink" it into the thread.

❏ If the design used was not digitized for foam you may need to repeat the stitching sequence to cover the foam adequately.

❏ Should there be any unsightly thread ends remaining, poke them to the back of the piece using a "Snag Nab It" Tool.

❏ Practice this technique, modifying these guidelines to suit your individual project, machine, motif and fabric. Always make a sample before stitching on a garment.

❏ Consider puffing embroidery designs, monograms and satin stitching columns on garments, hats, bags, wall hangings and decorative quilts.

STEPS TO PERFECT PUFFING

❏ Hoop and stabilize your project as usual.

❏ Drop the feed dogs on your sewing machine.

❏ Cut the Puffy Foam slightly larger than the design area to be puffed by determining the foam size and position from a design template. The foam is placed on top of the fabric and shouldn't extend over the hoop edges.

❏ If stitching "free-motion", attach a quilting/darning foot to your machine. This foot doesn't fit close to the throatplate and allows room for the foam. If computer embroidering, the embroidery foot naturally fits closely to the throatplate to prevent the hoop from bouncing during the stitching and may drag against the foam, if too thick, distorting the design.

❏ Adjust the presser foot pressure.

❏ Keep the upper tension light to prevent flattening the foam. The setting should be similar to that used when applying a buttonhole.

Note: The presser foot sensor may falsely signal on some machines when using the 3mm or 2 layers of 2mm to equal 4mm. Solution: use a single thickness of 2mm.

Reprinted with permission from **SEW NEWS Magazine.** For subscription information call 1-800-289-6397.

Making Matching Embroidered Socks

By Patti Jo Larson

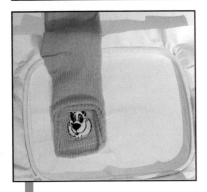

1. Hoop a piece of Sulky Sticky Stabilizer, shiny paper side up.

2. Score and peel back the paper from an area (approximately 3" square) near the center of the hoop.

3. Leaving the sock right side out, extend the cuff out flat and simply lay it on top of the exposed Sticky Stabilizer. Hand press it into place. (It doesn't matter if the toe of the sock is laying toward or away from you or off to the left, because you can rotate the design.) Just square it up as much as possible and it will be easy to match the pair.

4. You should now have the sock cuff held in place in the hoop. Of course, you do not want to embroider through both layers of the cuff, so simply roll back the top layer, exposing the right side of the cuff that the Sticky Stabilizer is holding. That (inside layer) is the one that will be embroidered. **5.** There are several ways to secure the top layer out of the way. Hold it with your fingers, use pins, or Patti Jo prefers to tack stitch it back by machine. **6.** With the top layer out of your way, use the positioning arrows to center the embroidery on the cuff. Simply touch and run the embroidery of your choice. Don't forget to use your small Puffy Foam scraps to make the embroidery on the socks stand out even more.

Remember ... First, the top edge of the cuff as it is extended out on the stabilizer in the hoop is actually the bottom of the cuff when it is turned down for wearing. Change the size of the embroidery by changing the stitch width and length. Second, to make a right and left sock you must place one sock on the Sticky with the toe pointing right and the other with the toe pointing left. Mirror image the embroidery on the sock.

To make these fun-to-wear matching outfits you will need:

✔ **"Hanes Her Way"™ Ready-to-Wear bright colored T-shirts, Shorts and matching Socks in Adult and Child's size.**

✔ **Husqvarna Viking #1+ or Rose and Embroidery Unit**
  • Braiding Foot
  • Bias Binder Foot
  • Edge Joining Foot
  • Bobbins

✔ **Machine Needles:**
  A new needle ---
  Top Stitching
  or Embroidery
  Size 14/90

✔ **Notions:**
  • Steam-A-Seam 2 Double-Sided, Fusible Web
  • Iron & Pressing Pad
  • Scissors & Pins
  • Rotary Cutter w/Wavy Blade, Ruler and Mat

✔ **2 mm Sulky Puffy Foam™ in a color to match the Sulky 30 wt. Rayon Thread**

✔ **Sulky Threads:**
  Sulky 30 wt. Rayon to coordinate with your fabric selection and Sulky Puffy Foam colors

  Sulky 40 wt. Rayon As listed on the embroidery card of your choice

  Sulky Clear Polyester Invisible Thread for the Bobbin or **Sulky White Bobbin Thread**

✔ **Sulky Stabilizers:**
  Totally Stable or **Sulky Sticky**

✔ **Tropical or primary colored fabrics**
  Joyce used Alexander Henry and Hoffman Prints, and Robert Kaufman's Pointillist Fabrics

Grandma Goes Wild

A Sulky Puffy Foam™ Project

By Joyce Drexler,
Creative Director for Sulky of America.
As shown on "America Sews with Sue Hausmann"
PBS TV, Program AM 501.

On a shopping trip with her 7 year old granddaughter, Amber, Joyce spotted brilliant-colored knitwear in adult's and children's sizes by Hanes "Her-Way"™. She envisioned these separates teamed with wild jungle and tropical fabrics and embellished with co-ordinating embroideries from the Husqvarna Viking Embroidery Library, and this project was conceived.

Step One: Choose Fabric for Blocks

Determine the color and size fabric blocks and placement on the T-shirt front (and back, if desired) for the size shirt you have chosen. Rough cut only the square you wish to embroider at this time. Joyce used the following finished sizes for the Adult and Child.

Adult - Size XL - 3 1/4" down from neck:
Base Rectangle	4 1/2" wide
Frame Square	3 1/2"
Embroidered Square	3"

Child - Size 7 - 1 1/4" down from neck:
Base Rectangle	4 1/2" wide
Frame Square	3 1/2"
Embroidered Square	3"

These measurements will depend
on the width of the shirt.

Step Two: Prepare to Embroider Motifs

1. After selecting your embroidery design and the solid or Pointillist dotted fabric on which to embroider the matching motifs, set up your machine for embroidery. For the Husqvarna Viking #1+ or Rose Sewing Machines:

a. Insert card and cassette.
b. Turn unit on.
c. Put on Embroidery Foot (Q for #1+, quilting position for Rose).
d. Set presser foot pressure for embroidery.
e. Drop feed teeth.
f. Thread machine with appropriate Sulky 40 Wt. Rayon Thread for your chosen design.
g. Use Sulky Polyester Bobbin Thread in the bobbin, threaded through the hole in the bobbin case.

2. Hoop fabric, layering stabilizer under fabric to be embroidered. If the piece of fabric is a scrap which is smaller than the hoop, iron a large piece of Totally Stable onto the back of the fabric and catch the edges of the stabilizer in the hoop, making sure the fabric is centered. Or, adhere Sulky Sticky to the underside of the hoop and press the fabric into it.

Clip hoop onto embroidery unit, touch stitch, check perimeters, adjust size (if you want a smaller motif for a smaller T-shirt, simply shorten stitch width and length before stitching), touch Run. When the design is finished, snip threads and remove stabilizer.

Step Three: Fuse Embroidered Square and Frame over Retangle

1. After embroidered squares are completed, begin the embellishment of the T-shirt front. Look at your novelty print and find elements in the design that would look good as a horizontal panel across the front of your T-shirt. Cut a rectangle of fabric about 6" high and 10" across, or wider, depending on how large your shirt is. Using Steam-A-Seam 2, double-sided paper-backed fusible web, remove the printed paper release sheet to reveal the tacky side; finger press it to the wrong side of your rectangle. (For a softer finished look, adhere fabrics by spraying the backs with Sulky KK 2000 temporary spray glue.) For a decorative effect, cut around the edges of the rectangle, *through the web,* with the aid of your ruler and wavy blade rotary cutter.

2. Place the rectangle on the T-shirt front, positioning it to your liking. Fuse it in place with a pressing motion (do not move the iron back and forth). This particular web will adhere to fabric and keep cut edges from fraying.

3. Back Pointillist Fabric with Steam-A- Steam 2. Cut these "frame" fabrics to 1/4-1/2" in from each other or whatever looks good and fits correctly when stacked on one another. Trim around the edges with the wavy rotary cutter. Fuse over the rectangular fabric panel.

4. Back the *embroidered* Pointillist Fabric piece(s) with web and trim with the wavy rotary cutter. Center in the previously-fused square(s) and fuse down with a steam iron. Turn the T-shirt inside out and fuse from the back as well.

Step Four: Stabilize where decorative satin stitching will be placed.

1. Iron 2 layers of Sulky Totally Stable or place 2 layers of Sulky Tear-Easy, cut in 2" strips, on the back of the T-shirt over the areas where more decorative stitching will be done over the Puffy Foam.

Hooped Embroidery with Sulky Puffy Foam on top of fabric

1. If you don't have a preprogrammed satin stitch on your machine, reduce the length way down to as short as it will go and still stitch. On the Husqvarna Viking computer sewing machines, select the medium satin stitch (A15). Place the Puffy Foam piece under the foot and satin stitch around the embroidered design and novelty print panel approximately 1/2" in from the scalloped, cut edge.
2. Tear away the excess foam. This foam was designed specifically for the sewing industry, so the perforation of the stitching will cause the excess to literally fall away from your work.

More Decorative Stitching with Puffy Foam

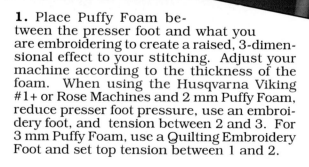

1. Place Puffy Foam between the presser foot and what you are embroidering to create a raised, 3-dimensional effect to your stitching. Adjust your machine according to the thickness of the foam. When using the Husqvarna Viking #1+ or Rose Machines and 2 mm Puffy Foam, reduce presser foot pressure, use an embroidery foot, and tension between 2 and 3. For 3 mm Puffy Foam, use a Quilting Embroidery Foot and set top tension between 1 and 2.

2. Another trick is to use a rotary cutter to cut a thin strip of 2 mm Puffy Foam 2 mm wide (for 3 mm foam, cut 3 mm wide). Insert the strip through the hole in the Braiding Foot and satin stitch over the foam tube to couch it onto the fabric. This makes turning corners cleaner and easier.

These techniques are particularly nice for kid's clothes because the Puffy effect is permanent through washings. It won't come off like puffy paints. **Do not, however, overheat in your dryer, or put direct pressure from a hot iron on puffed up stitching.**

Optional Cuff Embellishment

1. Rotary cut or tear a 5" wide crossgrain strip of wild print fabric.
2. To make cuffs, fold in half lengthwise, wrong sides together. Press.
3. To add the cuffs, open under-arm seams (or inseams on shorts) about 2" from bottom edge of hem.
4. Expose the free arm on your machine.
5. Leaving shirt right-side out, lay the folded cuff on the throat plate first and slip the sleeve over so the cuff is inside.
6. Line up the raw edges of the cuff to the folded edge of the existing sleeve hem. Sew together.
7. Repeat to add other cuff.

Fall Maple Leaves
A Sulky Puffy Foam™ Idea
by Lindee Goodall

The design for the Maple Leaf that is suitable for Puffy Foam, plus the "quilted" version that she used on the inside of the vest are both on "Fall 1", a digitized embroidery card designed by Lindee for her company, CACTUS PUNCH.

Lindee's Puffy Tips: • Tear the foam off before the final satin stitches are sewn; however, you can shoot the finished work with a burst of steam and it will cause those little "shreddies" to shrink away, if your iron is potent enough! • Puffy Foam works better on firmer, stiffer fabrics for two reasons: 1. Foam needs support to retain its dimension. 2. Foam designs have such high density which puts a lot of needle penetrations in the fabric, so they are not suitable for vinyl or leather.

The Vest: Lindee did three versions of the leaf. The dark green leaf was redesigned for a single color and better trimming efficiency. There are 3 sizes: 90%, 100%, and 110%. These she embroidered randomly. The Puffy Foam leaf version is in 2 sizes: 100% and 110%. She used 2mm Puffy Foam but the loftier 3mm will also look great. The third version of the leaf is a triple-stitch outline or quilting version used on the lining. Although there were 3 sizes of the leaf on the lining, she mainly used the largest size since you could not see a real difference due to the color of the fabric and thread.

To reduce the bulk, she used fleece instead of batting in the vest. The vest was lined and quilted mainly to give it more body and to eliminate the visibility of the Sulky Cut-Away Plus permanent stabilizer. The vest was finished with piping. Lindee says she suffers from "buttonhole phobia" so she improvised with twisted gold metallic thread for a loop and a perfect maple leaf button for the closure.

Vest modeled by Julie Drexler.

Lindee liked the fall Sulky variegated thread colors for the canvas bag. The Spring Tote Bag used 3 different colors and there are 4 colors on the Fall Versions plus Sulky Copper Metallic #7010 on the inside and the dark solid green on the outside.

Before embroidering, back the "flat" leaves with Sulky Tear-Easy for a soft feel and easy removability; use permanent Sulky "Cut-Away Plus" behind the foam leaves on the vest to help keep the fabric from pulling around the Foam.

Canvas tote bags are ideal for Puffy Designs since they are made of a firm fabric that is not likely to be laundered often.

You will need:

✔ **Canvas Tote Bag and/or firm woven fabric for Vest & Lining**
✔ **Fall #1 CACTUS PUNCH Embroidery Card**
✔ **Machine Needles:** Top Stitching or Embroidery Size 14/90
✔ **Sulky Puffy Foam**

✔ **Sulky 40 wt. Rayon Variegated Thread or solid colors for the needle and bobbin.**
✔ **Sulky Tear-Easy and Cut-Away Plus Stabilizers**
✔ **Vest Pattern - Fabric & Fleece**

• What? • When? • Where? • Why? & • How? to Sucessfully use ...

Sulky KK 2000™
Temporary Spray Adhesive

What is KK 2000?

*Sulky KK 2000 is the first and **only safe, non-flammable,** temporary spray adhesive on the market which temporarily bonds fabrics and fibers together, virtually eliminating pinning for appliqueing, embroidering, quilting, embellishing, stenciling and sewing. It contains a highly concentrated material and a heavier-than-air gas propellant that makes it **non-toxic and ozone friendly** (no CFC's or HCFC's) with an excellent spray nozzle for good directional flow to eliminate wasteful overspraying. It is odorless and colorless and doesn't leave any stains or residue.*

When would I use KK 2000 Temporary Spray Adhesive?

To enchance the quality of home embroidery, use KK 2000 to adhere stretchy knits to stabilizers, adhere Puffy Foam to fabric and to eliminate hoop marks. KK 2000 makes fabrics repositionable for applique, for trial fittings of hems, darts, pockets and shoulder pads, and to check positioning of embellishments like laces, trims, rick-rack, yarns, beads and buttons. Use it for quilt basting and to secure tear-away quilt patterns and templates for cutting and stitching.

Where would I use KK 2000 Temporary Spray Adhesive?

Sulky KK 2000 was originally developed for applique, but it also helps provide drum-tight hooping of stretch fabrics when sprayed onto the Sulky Stabilizer, allowing these fabrics to be placed in their own natural lie. This is particularly useful when dealing with large hoop areas. KK 2000 also helps stop warping of knit rows during embroidery, and it is great for "unhoopables" such as collars cut on the bias, pocket flaps, etc., as well as mending holes by spraying the damaged area together with a suitable backing.

Why would I use Sulky KK 2000 Temporary Spray Adhesive instead of other techniques or brands?

Use it while embroidering to significantly reduce the movement of stretchy or slippery material, to eliminate puckering, and to hold Sulky Puffy Foam in place. KK 2000 does not make fabric permanently stiff as other brands can. It completely absorbs into the fibers of the fabric within 24 to 36 hours and completely disappears within 2-5 days, while other spray adhesives remain stiff and fused, with white residue, many months after application.

KK 2000 has less gas and more glue in the can, up to 70% more usuable product than any other brand. Don't let the large cans fool you!

How would I use KK 2000 Temporary Spray Adhesive?

* Spray KK 2000 at a distance of 6" to 10", onto one surface only. Finger-press onto receiving surface, and you can stitch immediately without gumming up the needle.
* One short spray of KK 2000 is usually sufficient, while butane propelled adhesives usually need the equivalent of 2 or more cloud-producing sprays that can float out into your room.
* Spray KK 2000 on the back of fabric applique pieces to make them repositionable.
* Spray KK 2000 onto any and all of the Sulky Stabilizers (except Heat-Away) to make them a self-stick stabilizer to embroider difficult-to-hoop items like pockets, edges, button rows, ribbons, cuffs, collars, socks, neckties, linen, silk handkerchiefs, doll clothes, etc., as well as for counted cross stitch, silk ribbon work, and hand embroidery in a hoop.
* Spray KK 2000 on either tear-away quilt patterns, templates, or stencils to hold them in place while stitching or stenciling.
* Use KK 2000 on paper patterns for easy tracing and cutting.
* Always spray away from the machine or machine parts.

KK 2000™

45

Read through all instructions before starting this project. If you are using a computerized cutwork design, stitch out a sample to verify both the stitching order and when it would be appropriate to stop the embroidery process to cut the fabric layers.

You will need:

- ✔ **Sulky Soft 'n Sheer Stabilizer**
- ✔ 1 - 27" x 45" fabric for pillowcase
- ✔ 1 - 13" x 45" fabric for band of pillowcase
- ✔ 1 1/2 yds of self-made or purchased piping
- ✔ Sulky 40 wt. Rayon Thread Colors:
    #1108 - Lt. Mauve
    #1256 - Sweet Pink
- ✔ Sulky Bobbin Thread, white
- ✔ Size 75 Embroidery Needles
- ✔ Husqvarna Viking #1+ Machine
- ✔ Huskylock 1002 LCD Serger
- ✔ Accessory Piping Foot for Serger
- ✔ Husqvarna Viking Embroidery Card #20, Design #4
- ✔ #1+ Embroidery Hoop
- ✔ Curved 4" Embroidery Scissors
- ✔ Applique Scissors
- ✔ Electric Stencil Cutter or low temp. soldering iron (not over 650 degrees)
- ✔ 8 1/2" x 11" piece of glass

Instructions:

1. With wrong sides together, fold the 13" x 45" fabric to form a 6 1/2" x 45" strip of fabric. The embroidery will be sewn through both layers.

2. Exclusive of seam allowances, quarter the fabric to determine the design center. Remember, there are seam allowances on both the length and width of the fabric.

3. Press a faint line to mark the horizontal and vertical centers of the design to facilitate placement in the hoop.

4. With the fold of the fabric on the right side of the hoop, place the fabric with **Soft 'n Sheer Stabilizer** under it in the Plus Hoop, making sure that the vertical and horizontal centers of the fabric are properly aligned.

5. Set your Husqvarna Viking #1+ for embroidery using Embroidery Card #20, Design #4.

6. Sulky 40 wt. Rayon Thread #1108 Lt. Mauve and #1256 Sweet Pink were used on the top for this project, with White Sulky Bobbin Thread in the bobbin.

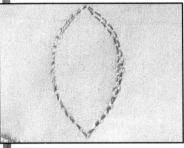

7. Stitch out just the first anchoring stitches of the design, then remove the hoop from the embroidery arm. **DO NOT UNHOOP THE FABRIC.**

8. Using curved embroidery scissors and applique scissors, carefully cut away both layers of fabric, one layer at a time, inside the stitching lines as close to the stitching line as possible. Remember that the satin stitching has to cover this raw edge. **DO NOT CUT THROUGH THE STABILIZER.**

9. Reattach the hoop to the machine and continue sewing the embroidery, removing the hoop, cutting away fabric inside stitching lines, and reattaching the hoop to complete the remainder of the design.

Cutwork Pillowcase

*A Sulky Soft 'n Sheer™
Cut-Away Permanent
Stabilizer Project*

"There is nothing as elegant or breathtaking as exquisite cutwork. Crisp, clean lines add to the beauty of this art form, but the trick is in achieving perfect lines.

Technology today has given us computerized cutwork, and Sulky Cut-Away Stabilizers have refined the process even more. Unlike tear-aways and wash-aways, the cut-away stabilizer becomes a permanent part of the cutwork, lending durability, longevity and a flawless finish to your garment.

Whether you are doing cutwork by computerized embroidery machine or with a zig-zag stitch on your sewing machine, Sulky Soft 'n Sheer Cut-Away Stabilizer will truly enchance the quality and beauty of your sewing." --- Donna

Donna Hoeflinger
*of Sugar Land, TX
Designer, Educator*

The Girl Scout sewing merit badge is what first stimulated Donna's interest in sewing, and she has been sewing ever since. She was an avid sewer when her children were small, and today she even sews for her "fur children", JJ and Cindy.

After working in the medical field for many years, Donna has started a second career in sewing and now enjoys teaching as a Freelance Educator for the Husqvarna Viking Sewing Machine Co. She works diligently as a volunteer for the American Sewing Guild, and serves on its Advisory Board. She was Hospitality Chairman for the 1997 ASG National Convention in Houston, TX. Donna has published two books, Back to Basics and Back to Basics, Jr. In addition, Donna taught at the International Husqvarna Viking 1997 Annual Convention in Orlando, Florida.

10. When the design has finished sewing, remove the hoop from the embroidery arm, **BUT DO NOT UNHOOP THE FABRIC.** Trim all threads from the top and reverse side of embroidery.

11. With the fabric still hooped, place the embroidery on the 8 1/2" x 11" glass. Use the fine point tip of the stencil cutter to burn away the stabilizer within the open areas. Cut away the excess stabilizer from back of design.

12. Remove the cutwork band from the hoop. With right sides together, serge a seam on both 13" sides of the fabric.

13. With wrong sides together, refold fabric to make a fabric tube.

14. For this project, fuchsia tulle was placed over pink satin and wrapped over 1/8" filler cord to make the piping.

15. To facilitate making the piping, a piping foot was used on the Huskylock 1002 LCD serger. Using the 27" x 45" piece of fabric, attach piping to a 45" side of the fabric. With right sides together, serge a seam on the bottom and open side of the pillowcase. With right sides together, match raw edges of the band and pillowcase, then serge a final seam.

Dimensional Embroidery

A Cut-Away Soft 'n Sheer™ and Cut-Away Plus™ Permanent Stabilizers Project

"I chose Soft 'n Sheer for this project because it is soft, yet it will support the stitches without adding stiffness. It trims away cleanly from the stitched edge and can even be 'burned' away because of its nylon consistency." --- Patsy

Patsy Shields

Sellersburg, IN

National Director of Education for Sulky of America

Patsy has traveled extensively throughout the U.S. for over 15 years as a free-lance sewing specialist teaching serger classes, fitting workshops, and machine art seminars.

She has been published in the SERGER UPDATE NEWSLETTER and has contributed both to a book for the SINGER REFERENCE LIBRARY and to SEW NEWS, as well as co-authoring the UPDATED SERGER CONCEPTS IN SULKY BOOK and the PATCHWORK CONCEPTS IN SULKY BOOK.

She has taught at National Sewing Events including SMART, BABY LOCK TECH, NEW HOME INSTITUTE, QUILT MARKET AND QUILT FESTIVAL as well as SULKY INSTRUCTOR TRAINING SEMINARS and over a hundred Sulky "SEW EXCITING"™ SEMINARS.

As National Director of Education for Sulky of America, she coordinates Sulky's Educational Activity at trade shows and consumer shows as well as training Sulky Free-lance Educators to conduct "Sew Exciting Seminars".

You will need:

✔ **Sulky Cut-Away Plus**
✔ **Sulky Cut-Away Soft 'n Sheer**
✔ Computerized Embroidery Machine
✔ Favorite Embroidery Card (project design came from Baby Lock Card #14, Large Florals, stitched on the Esante II).
✔ Machine Embroidery Hoop
✔ Sulky 40 wt. Rayon Threads

1. Place the Soft 'n Sheer Cut-Away Stabilizer in your sewing machine's embroidery hoop and stitch only the parts of the flowers that you plan to be 3-D. Do not stitch the last bit of color in the flower centers. Remove the stabilizer from the hoop. Cut out the flowers close to the stitching.

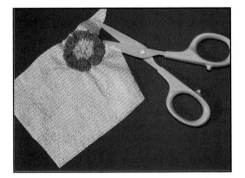

2. Place the fabric to be embroidered, with Cut-Away Plus under it, into the embroidery hoop and stitch the design, except for the last dot of color in flower centers. Place the dimensional flowers on carefully, aligning everything up properly; use Sulky KK 2000 Temporary Spray Adhesive to hold flowers in place; stitch the last dot of color in flower centers to secure them. These 3-D overlays will lift up and add extra pizzazz to your project.

3. Remove fabric from the hoop, cut away the stabilizer, and make into a picture, pillow or garment inset.

Cross Stitch Keepsake Box

A Sulky Soft 'n Sheer™ and KK 2000™ Project Idea
by Jane Bowers Nesbit

"I love this stabilizer because it gives the stabilization of a heavy, thick stabilizer, but it is lightweight and supple." --- Jane

You will need:
- ✔ "Adornables" Counted Cross Stitch Kit
- ✔ **Sulky Soft 'n Sheer Permanent Stabilizer**
- ✔ **Sulky KK 2000 Temporary Spray Adhesive**
- ✔ 40 wt. Rayon Thread
- ✔ Hot Glue Gun
- ✔ Sulky White Bobbin Thread
- ✔ Pfaff Fantasy Card #14
- ✔ Pfaff Creative 7570 and Fantasy Unit
- ✔ Size 80 Hoop
- ✔ Embroidery Foot
- ✔ Size 80 Universal Needle

Jane Bowers Nesbit
Pfaff Training Manager

Jane joined Pfaff in 1983 as an Educational Consultant, traveling the United States teaching and promoting Pfaff Sewing Machines. She became a Pfaff Sales Rep in 1985 and held that position until 1989 when she became the National Training Manager responsible for training Pfaff personnel and dealers on new products. Jane also co-organizes Pfaff's Conventions and National Shows. She has appeared on several cable TV shows with HGTV personalities Carol Duval and Kitty Bartholomew. Jane believes that if a person can sew, a person can be stress-free.

Instructions:
1. Lightly spray **Sulky Soft 'n Sheer** with Sulky KK 2000 Temporary Spray Adhesive, and firmly press a 6" x 6" cross stitch cloth on top of it. Hoop in the size 80 hoop. Make sure to keep the grain lines straight without stretching.
2. Set up your Machine for Programmed Machine Embroidery. Thread the top with the first of your Rayon Thread color choices. Put Sulky White Bobbin Thread in the bobbin.
3. Select cross stitch design. Use the Pfaff Fantasy Card #14, program #10 at its largest size.
4. Sew out the cross stitch design with your 40 wt. Rayon color choices.
5. Trim **Soft 'n Sheer** close to design and press.
6. Finish box according to the directions on the "Adornables" package.

T-Shirt Dress Embellishment

A Sulky Soft 'n Sheer Permanent Stabilizer Project

Debi Kuennen-Baker

Pfaff Educational Consultant

Debi lives in California but travels extensively teaching dealers and consumers about Pfaff products. She won first place in the first Pfaff E.C. Contest and she has been winning awards every since. Debi has had several items featured in the Pfaff Club Magazine.

"I prefer Sulky Soft 'n Sheer on t-shirt, sweatshirt and sweater knits because of the way it controls the stretch of the knit. It also keeps the embroidery from stretching and sagging during wearing and washing, while remaining soft so it doesn't irritate the skin" --- Debi

You will need:

✔ 9" x 9" **Soft 'n Sheer Permanent Stabilizer**
✔ Pfaff Fantasy Cards 1, 4, and 22
✔ Pfaff Creative 7570 and Creative Fantasy Unit
✔ Size 120 Hoop or Pfaff Big Hoop
✔ Embroidery Foot
✔ Sulky KK 2000 Temporary Spray Adhesive
✔ Rayon Thread in colors appropriate for your chosen design
✔ Size 12/80 Universal Needle
✔ T-Shirt Dress

Instructions:

1. Mark the center placement of where you want the design to be placed. Hoop the **Soft 'n Sheer Stabilizer** and lightly spray the top of it with **Sulky KK-2000;** firmly press the T-shirt dress onto it, keeping center lines straight. Select a children's design (we used the Pfaff Fantasy Card #22, Program #12). Rotate design 180°. With right cursor arrow, enter move screen and move design to upper center. Thread the top with the first 40 wt. Rayon Thread color indicated by your design. Put a white bobbin thread in your bobbin. Place hoop in machine with the

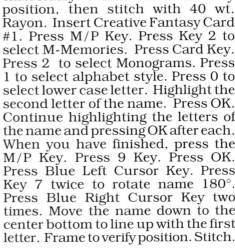

design facing the desired direction. Sew out the design with your selection of 40 wt. Rayon colors

2. Insert Fantasy Card #4. Select first letter of the name. Press Blue Right Cursor Key one time. Move the letter down to the bottom, positioned so the rest of the name will fit and be centered below the embroidery. Frame stitch to verify position, then stitch with 40 wt. Rayon. Insert Creative Fantasy Card #1. Press M/P Key. Press Key 2 to select M-Memories. Press Card Key. Press 2 to select Monograms. Press 1 to select alphabet style. Press 0 to select lower case letter. Highlight the second letter of the name. Press OK. Continue highlighting the letters of the name and pressing OK after each. When you have finished, press the M/P Key. Press 9 Key. Press OK. Press Blue Left Cursor Key. Press Key 7 twice to rotate name 180°. Press Blue Right Cursor Key two times. Move the name down to the center bottom to line up with the first letter. Frame to verify position. Stitch.

3. Remove hoop from machine. Trim Soft 'n Sheer close to design; the remainder stays behind the design to keep it from sagging during washings and wearings. Press from the back with a hot iron.

Note: When combining letters from two cards, sew out a test sample first so everything centers perfectly.

Lindee Goodall
of Tucson, AZ

Lindee Goodall and her husband, Bill, own Cactus Punch, an embroidery digitizing company recently relocated to Tucson, AZ. Lindee designs and teaches while Bill handles the machines and custom embroidery production jobs. For their efforts in assisting other embroiderers, they were recently named Embroiderer of the Month by The Embroidery Trade Association. They were interviewed by Embroidery Business News in their "Greatful Threads Tour." They have also contributed articles to Stitches Magazine. At METS 97, Lindee won first place for best original digitized design with a cutwork angel, and she has also been nominated for Impressions Magazine's "Digitizers of Distinction".

Sunflower Vest

A Sulky Heat-Away Stabilizer Idea

The Sunflower Vest is a combination of machine embroidery and sewing machine work which was inspired by a recent presentation by Patsy Shields. This vest uses Sulky Variegated Rayon Thread. For the dragonfly on the back, a cross-hatching technique with a low density was used to achieve that translucent iridescent look of real dragonfly wings. The digitized three-dimensional sunflowers are soft and touchable because they were created on Heat-Away Brush-Off Stabilizer. The embroidery designs from this vest are on the Cactus Punch "Spring Things 1" Disk.

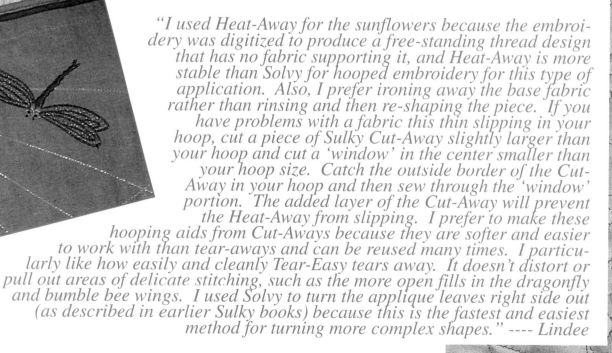

"I used Heat-Away for the sunflowers because the embroidery was digitized to produce a free-standing thread design that has no fabric supporting it, and Heat-Away is more stable than Solvy for hooped embroidery for this type of application. Also, I prefer ironing away the base fabric rather than rinsing and then re-shaping the piece. If you have problems with a fabric this thin slipping in your hoop, cut a piece of Sulky Cut-Away slightly larger than your hoop and cut a 'window' in the center smaller than your hoop size. Catch the outside border of the Cut-Away in your hoop and then sew through the 'window' portion. The added layer of the Cut-Away will prevent the Heat-Away from slipping. I prefer to make these hooping aids from Cut-Aways because they are softer and easier to work with than tear-aways and can be reused many times. I particularly like how easily and cleanly Tear-Easy tears away. It doesn't distort or pull out areas of delicate stitching, such as the more open fills in the dragonfly and bumble bee wings. I used Solvy to turn the applique leaves right side out (as described in earlier Sulky books) because this is the fastest and easiest method for turning more complex shapes." ---- Lindee

Creative Lace Blouse

A Sulky Heat-Away™ Disintegrating Stabilizer Project

"I chose Sulky Heat-Away to make my thread lace because of its firmness; it worked best to keep the decorative stitches true to shape and I could remove it easily without disturbing delicate stitches." --- Carol

To make this designer lace blouse Carol used:

✔ **Sulky Heat-Away Stabilizer**
✔ Sulky 40 wt. Rayon Thread #1094 Med. Turquoise
✔ White Tulle Netting
✔ McCalls Pattern #8698 or other blouse pattern that has a front and/or back yoke
✔ Cherrywood Fabric
✔ New Home Memory Craft 9000
✔ Memory Card #107
✔ 7" Spring Tension Hoop
✔ Cloth Setter
✔ Washable Marker
✔ Darning Foot

Modeled by Patti Lee

Carol McKinney
Designer, Fiber Artist, Teacher
of Pasadena, TX

Carol designs and markets patterns for wearable art cut-work vests. She lives in Pasadena, Texas, with her husband Ricky and their two children, Lyndsi and Kimberly.

Carol has always loved sewing. Seven years ago, she started teaching classes in a local fabric store on the construction of cut-work vests, which led to her designing career. She currently teaches classes in Houston and the surrounding areas. In 1995, she designed a project and taught a class on it at New Home Convention. In the 1996 Sulky Challenge, her entry won third place and in 1997, her entry won first place in the Wearable Art Category.

Instructions:

Cut Tulle and Sulky Heat-Away slightly larger than the pattern pieces that you choose to make into lace inserts (in Carol's example, left front yoke, lace strip on front, and back yoke). Place the tulle on top of the Heat-Away and hoop as one.

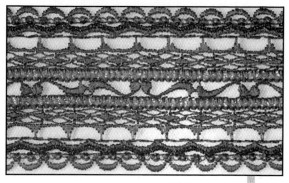

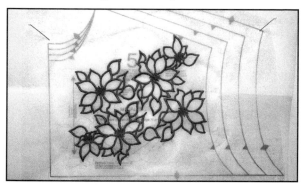

1. On the left front yoke and back yoke, use the cloth setter and templates to stitch 2-4 connected patterns from the memory card in a shape that is complimentary to these pattern pieces.

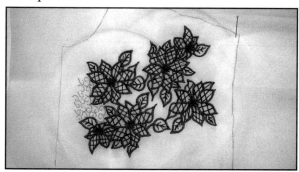

2. To define the area for squiggle stitching, use a washable marker to trace the cutting line of the pattern piece on the tulle, then draw the squiggle lines to fill in around the embroidered design as well as the richelieu bars within the flowers.

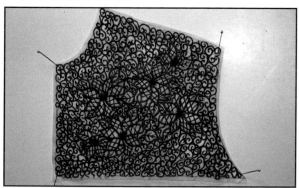

3. Attach a darning foot, lower feed dogs, set for free-motion straight stitch, thread top and bobbin with Sulky 40 wt #1094 Med. Turquoise, and insert the first part of the design in a 7" spring hoop. Follow the squiggle lines and the richelieu bar lines, going over them 3, 4 even 5 times, until the line is as heavy as you want it. Repeat until entire pattern piece is completed.

4. Following the package directions, remove the Heat-Away from each lace piece, ironing from the wrong side. These pieces are now ready for use in the garment.

5. To create a lace strip, place the tulle on top of the Heat-Away. Put Sulky Thread in the needle and bobbin, and use the decorative stitches on your machine to create the panel. Start stitching in the center, then place rows of stitching on both sides until the panel is as wide as you want it. Remove the Heat-Away per package directions.

6. To do the crosshatching that texturizes the fabric for the collar and sleeves, use a 1.6 mm twin needle with Sulky 40 wt. Thread #1094 Med. Turquoise in both needles and the bobbin.

Congratulations!
First Place Winner
in the 1997 Sulky
Wearable Art Challenge.
Designed by Carol McKinney using some of the same techniques as she used in this beautiful blouse project.

Spinning Bobbin Lace by Machine

A Sulky Heat-Away Stabilizer Project Idea

Sharee Dawn Roberts
Author, Designer, Instructor
Paducah, KY

Sharee Dawn Roberts received her Fine Arts Degree in Textile Design from San Diego University. She has received both national and international recognition for her high fashion quilted clothing and special machine art techniques. She was invited to Japan in 1988 to demonstrate her special skills, and she traveled to Australia to give seminars in April, 1993.

Sharee was the recipient of awards in the American Quilter's Society Fashion Show for three consecutive years and she was the grand prize winner in both 1987 and 1988. She placed First in the Fabric Fantasies Annual Juried Fabric Festival at Bazaar Del Mundo, San Diego, CA in 1990 and 1991. She has been a designer for the prestigious Fairfield Fashion Show for 1988, 1989, 1990, 1992 and 1994. Her clothing has been shown in galleries and exhibitions throughout the United States, Japan and Europe.

Sharee has been a contributing editor for THE AMERICAN QUILTER and THREADS magazines for several years, and she has designed a line of patterns. Her first book, CREATIVE MACHINE ART, was released in April, 1992. She is the owner of "Web of Threads", a mail-order business specializing in decorative threads for the Needlearts.

"Lacemaking is one of the oldest and most favorite forms of needleart, for obvious reasons. Lace is gorgeous! Whether it is crocheted like filigree or delicate strands of interwoven silk, there is something about the way beautiful threads are spun together in lacy patterns that intrigues those of us who love textiles. We want to touch it because it is nearly impossible to fully appreciate the tactile quality of lace without physically feeling it!

Now, with Sulky Heat-Away Stabilizer, it is possible to create on the sewing machine, using a simple, free-motion straight stitch, the most stunning lace for beautiful cutwork, inserts, collars and appliques for art-to-wear clothing. Your hands will spin intricate designs using shimmering Sulky Metallic and shiny, lustrous Sulky Rayon Threads. The lace you create will rival the most expensive, imported lace you have ever seen."
--- Sharee

You will need:

- Sulky Heat-Away Stabilizer
- Machine Embroidery Needles
  Size 11/75 and 14/90; Top Stitching
  Needle size 14/90 or 16/100
- Sulky 30 and 40 wt. Rayon Threads
- Sulky Original Metallic Threads
- Sulky Sliver™ Metallic Threads
- Optional - Machine Embroidery Hoop

The threads listed above are all machine embroidery threads which may be threaded through the sewing machine needle's eye. Other, heavier weight threads may be used as well, to be pulled from the bobbin. The advantage of combining the heavy threads with the machine embroidery threads is that the play of texture between the different weights is particularly pretty. Also, the heavier threads will build up the design more quickly and provide a more durable lace.

Bobbin Drawing:

Use the bobbin winder on your sewing machine to wind these thicker threads onto several empty bobbins. Do not use the tension guides on the machine; rather, pinch the cord between your thumb and forefinger to provide manual tension so that it winds tightly onto the empty bobbin. Try yarns from ON THE SURFACE, DESIGNER THREADS, RAYON OR METALLIC RIBBON FLOSS, etc.

Ready to Spin! The "trick" to creating beautiful lace with your sewing machine is largely understanding your materials (specialty threads and stabilizers) and your sewing machine's tension settings (both top and bobbin). The actual technique is very simple. But it is important to know which threads to use and how, and to practice adjusting your tensions to get the stitch that you desire.

No matter what you use in the bobbin, always use *machine embroidery threads* on the top of your machine. Even if you are sewing "upside down" (for bobbin drawing), you still want the threads to be beautiful on either side of your lace. The decision as to what threads to use is not an easy choice because practically anything is beautiful! Try mixing strongly colored Sulky 40 wt. variegated Rayon Threads with shiny Sulky Metallics and heavier top-stitching silk threads. Don't try to co-ordinate your thread colors because the most intriguing surprises occur when you combine different color families together!

You can either use machine embroidery thread in your bobbin or one of the heavier threads (yarns) to be used for bobbin drawing with the **back of your lace facing up.** Fill several bobbins with decorative yarn as they use up very quickly.

Use a regular foot with the feed dogs up for these first lines of straight stitching which will help to stabilize the Heat-Away so that you won't have to stretch it in a hoop once you switch to free-motion. Just sew several rows of stitching full speed, until you have spaced all lines of stitching approximately 1 1/2" apart.

To fill in spaces more quickly, using no pivoting, switch to free-motion; drop the feed dogs, put on a darning foot, and use a top-stitching or Metallic needle whenever you are using metallic threads.

The stitching is simple really, you can't go wrong. Using a straight stitch, simply slide the Heat-Away around over the bed of the machine to create loopy swirls of embroidery. Make sure that the thread loops connect (touch each other) so that when you remove the stabilizer, the lace will hold together. Do not make your stitching too dense, which is easy to do, as it goes very quickly! You may want to experiment with a small scrap first, to see what it will look like when the stabilizer is removed. Follow package instructions to disintegrate your Heat-Away, and you will be left with the most gorgeous lace ever!

Blouse created by Sharee Dawn Roberts. Modeled by Patti Lee.

"Sulky Embroidered Sealife Magnets, Pins and Clips"

A Sulky Heat-Away™ or Super Solvy Project

by Joyce Drexler as presented on the PBS TV Program "Sew Creative" with Donna Wilder.

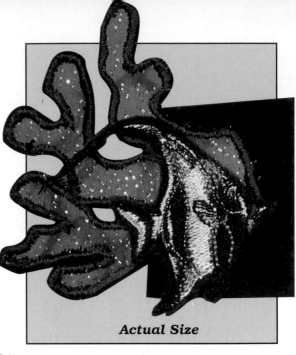

Actual Size

Embroidered Sealife, of course, goes great on clothing too. Modeled by Adam Drexler.

To make Sealife Magnets, etc. you will need:

✔ **A Zig-Zag Sewing Machine** with Computer Embroidery capabilities. We used New Home Card #104
✔ **Machine Needle:** Embroidery and Metallic size 90/14
✔ **Sulky Threads:** Sulky 40 wt. Rayon colors for Embroidery Design chosen and additional Sulky Rayons, Metallics and Sliver Metallic for Sea Grasses, plus Sulky Bobbin Thread.

✔ **Sulky Stabilizers:** Sulky Heat-Away™, Sulky Super Solvy™ and Sulky Sticky™
✔ **Fabrics:** Brown Felt Squares Black Ultra Suede Squares Fleece for padded seaweed
✔ **Magnets by the Sheet**
✔ **Extra-Fine, Permanent-Ink Marker**
✔ **6" German Hardwood Embroidery Hoop**
✔ **Fabric Glue - E-6000**
✔ **Iron and Teflon Pressing Sheet**
✔ **Dark Brown Felt**

---

1. Embroider Sealife Designs

Place a piece of Sulky Sticky in your machine's embroidery hoop and score it with a pin to remove the release paper. Finger press a square of Felt onto the stabilizer. Follow machine instructions for computer embroidery. Remove the stabilizer and trim felt up to the embroidery.

2. Make your own "Thread Fabric Lace"

Secure an 8" square of Heat-Away in a 6" embroidery hoop. Set your machine for "free-motion" embroidery:
• Lower or cover feed dogs
• Remove Presser Foot
• Reduce Top Tension

Thread your machine with a variegated or multi-colored Sulky Rayon in the needle and bobbin. Using a straight stitch, make free-motion circles or "e" shapes or, for a faster work-up, use an open satin stitch at a wide width. Have fun with this and add some Sulky 30 wt. Rayon and Sliver Metallic. The idea is to have an open lacy effect, not a solid fill-in.

3. Satin Stitch around the outer edge of the Sea Grass design line.

With a marker either free-hand draw your own grass design or trace our design onto the Thread Lace. Use the same thread in the bobbin and needle (I used Sulky Rayon

#1035 - Dark Burgundy), and a small width to satin stitch over the design lines. Disintegrate and remove the Heat-Away by pressing the wrong side with a dry, hot iron. Cut out the Sea Grass along the design lines and sandwich it between 2 layers of Solvy or Super Solvy. Press it for several seconds with a dry iron at a cotton setting. If your iron does not have a non-stick sole plate, use a teflon pressing sheet. Heavily stitch over the satin stitch again using a little wider width. Remove the Solvy and you have "Thread Lace" Sea Grass. See the next page for more ideas.

4. Make Padded Fabric Sea Grass

Sandwich cotton batting between two layers of a blue-green fabric with each right side out. Set machine for regular sewing. Choose a honey-comb stitch. Thread top with Sulky Sliver Metallic Opalescent #8040 and a color matching the fabric in the bobbin. Run rows of stitching next to one another, just touching.

Set up for "free-motion". Hoop the stitched work and select a small width to satin stitch a Sea Grass shape using a Sulky Rayon in the top and bobbin to match the fabric. Finish as in #3, trimming away fabric, sandwiching design between Solvy, satin stitching with a wider zig-zag, and removing the Solvy.

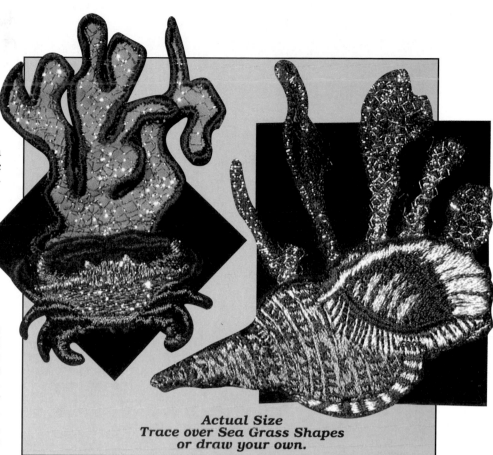

Actual Size
Trace over Sea Grass Shapes
or draw your own.

You can also make Embroidered Motifs & Sea Grass into Pins, Vest Cinchers, Hair Clips etc.

5. Assemble the Magnet

Cut Black Ultra Suede into a square the size desired for the motif. Finger press to a sticky-back magnet sheet. Cut the magnet sheet to the size of the Ultra Suede. Using E-6000 glue or a hot glue gun, glue your Sea Grass to the Ultra Suede. Then, glue the embroidered Fish or Shell over the Sea Grass.

Instead of gluing to a magnet base, glue Ultra Suede to a template of cardboard, plastic, or Fimo™ Clay. Then glue a pin-back onto it.

To make a vest cincher, do not add the Ultra Suede square, instead, just tack-stitch your Sea Life motif and Sea Grass to a Vest Cincher, then make an embroidered vest to match!

Try adding your embroidered Sea Life to a half-folded pin-woven square and use it as a lapel wrap-style pin. Add some hanging twisted yarns and Sulky Threads behind the Sea Grass for an even more designer-art look.

Let your imagination take over...you may find the "mind play" result very interesting!

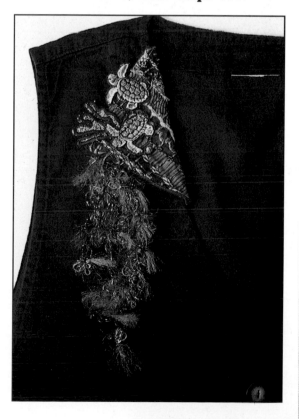

"Classy" Crochet Edge

A Sulky Heat-Away™ Disintegrating Stabilizer Project

"I preferred Sulky Heat-Away Stabilizer for this project because I needed crisp stability to support multiple rows of crochet stitching off the edge of the fabric. I also like how you can see the stitching on the Heat-Away (easier than on clear Solvy) so it is easier to line up the rows of stitching." --- Sue

Add an heirloom crochet or tatted edge to collars, cuffs, necklines, ruffles and more. It took our Grandmothers days to make a project with this delicate technique. But today, thanks to Sulky Threads and Heat-Away Stabilizer, and quick sewing machine techniques, we stitch it in an hour or so.

Add this designer detail to update a blouse or suit by stitching the crochet or tatted edge around a collar as I did on this washed rayon dress. Or, turn an edge and topstitch or hemstitch, then add the crochet along the finished edge. Heirloom embroideries complete the look. The beautiful bows on my dress are Martha Pullen designs from Husqvarna Viking Embroidery Card # 11.

Sue Hausmann

Hostess of the PBS-TV show "America Sews with Sue Hausmann" and Vice President of Husqvarna Viking Sewing Machine Co.

Sue's teaching prowess equals her sewing ability and, for more than 20 years, her profession has focused on sewing education. In presenting a variety of motivational sewing seminars, she demonstrates to retailers and consumers that sewing is fast and, above all, fun!

Sue has produced numerous instructional videos for consumers about basic sewing machine and serger operation, as well as creative options. As Vice President for Husqvarna Viking, she oversees the education and training programs for consumers, as well as retail store owners and their employees. She is also intensely involved with consumer motivation programs and new product development.

With more than 100 public broadcasting programs and nine books to her credit, Sue is realizing her dream to share the joy of sewing. Her enthusiasm motivates sewers, and would-be sewers, to complete America Sews' projects with confidence.

To make a Classy Crochet Edge by machine you will need:

✔ **Sulky Heat-Away Stabilizer**
✔ Sulky 30 wt. Rayon Thread
✔ Topstitching Needle
✔ Edge/Joining Presser Foot
✔ Open Toe Presser Foot

Instructions:

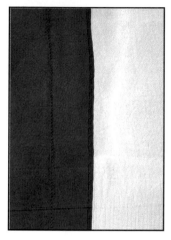
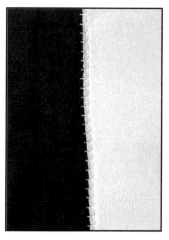

1. To make the heavier, crochet-look trim, thread the top of your sewing machine with two strands of the same color of Sulky 30 wt. Rayon Thread through the eye of a topstitching needle. Also treat the two threads as one to wind a bobbin with two strands of the same Sulky 30 wt. thread.

2. Rotary cut strips of Heat-Away Stabilizer 3 inches wide. Snap on the edge/joining foot and baste the Heat-Away strips onto the fabric along the edge with 2 inches extending outside the fabric edge to be finished with "crochet".

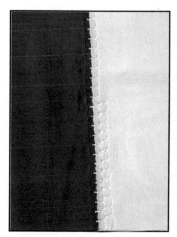

3. Select a stitch that sews a seam/overcast-type stitch. On a Husqvarna Viking #1+, use stitch A21, stitch length 3.0, stitch width 6.0, side-to-side mirror image, and an open-toe foot.

4. Stitch along the edge of the collar so the side stitch catches the edge, and the rest of the stitch is on the Heat-Away. To finish the ends, select a left needle (or right needle depending on which end) and straight stitch on the Heat-Away to the next row. Mirror the stitch side-to-side, turn the work around, and stitch back along the stitching. Line up the stitch with the side stitches of this row between the side stitches of the first row. The stitches should look like you are laying brick. Continue to add rows as desired. The collar in the sample project has three rows.

5. Trim away the excess Heat-Away outside the stitching.

6. Place a towel or press cloth on an ironing surface and press with a DRY iron to disintegrate the Heat-Away.

7. Place the collar in a plastic bag and rub the stitching gently to "flake" the Heat-Away off.

You have an heirloom garment that looks like it took days to create. *Enjoy!*

Sue's Hint:

"I have an old travel iron, purchased at a garage sale, that is perfect for this because it has no steam holes. It turns the Heat-Away a scorched color quickly."

"Circular Faux Woven Scarf or Vest"

A Sulky Heat-Away or Super Solvy Project

Presented on PBS TV - by Joyce Drexler
for "America Sews with Sue Hausmann".
Original Idea from an article in
"Threads Magazine" by Yvonne Perez-Collins.

Brenda Duncan
of Atlanta, GA
A Sulky "Sew Exciting
Seminar"
National Educator

Brenda was born and raised in England at a time when learning to sew and knit was as basic as reading and writing. Upon moving to the United States in 1971, Brenda immediately became involved in the sewing industry teaching classes on clothing construction and machine techniques for a well-known sewing machine manufacturer. She worked at a local sewing store and considers it to have been an invaluable opportunity to increase her knowledge in this field. Currently Brenda teaches "Sulky Sew Exciting" Seminars throughout the South on a variety of machine and decorative thread techniques.

"Pin Weaving cords, ribbons and strips of fabric to make a fabric that can be used in different projects has become an ever-growing trend. Brenda has taken the look of pin-weaving and combined it with the ease of working with Sulky Heat-Away Disintegrating Stabilizer and machine stitching with Sulky Invisible, or any of Sulky's Decorative Threads, to create an illusion of weaving. Quicker and easier than actual pin-weaving. The Scarf is an easy, quick project that you can complete in approximately 3 hours. Makes a perfect gift ---one size fits all!" --- Brenda

To make this beautiful Faux Woven Scarf you will need:

✔ **A Zig-Zag Sewing Machine** with one or more of the following attachments, depending on type of yarn used:
  • Wide and/or Narrow Braiding Foot,
  • 5 or 7 Hole Cording Foot if you want to make your own cord.
  • Ribbon Foot
  • Piping Foot
  • Open-toe Applique Foot
  • Felt Pad for Spool Pin

✔ **Machine Needle:**
  • Size 80/12 or 90/14

✔ **Sulky Threads:**
Sulky 30 wt. Rayon
  • 1192 - Fuchsia
Sulky Sliver™ Metallic
  • 8007 - Gold
Sulky Clear Invisible Polyester Thread
in the Needle and Bobbin

✔ **Sulky Stabilizers:**
1 package of either
Sulky Heat-Away™ or
Sulky Super Solvy™

✔ **ON THE SURFACE™ Decorative Yarns for weavers:**
(see Sources p.137)
  • 5 yds. of #1 from card #SGT116
  • 10 yds. each of #3, #5 & #6 from card #DGT115
  • 5 yds. of #1 from card #SGT116

✔ **Rayon Flat Braid in a Hand-Dyed Multi-Color** (see Sources p.137)
30-35 yds. Yarn steps color - Sunset Blvd.
(See Cover for another color)

✔ **Notions:**
  • Teflon and Cloth Pressing Sheets
  • Iron & Pressing Pad
  • Pinking Shears or Pinking Rotary Cutter, Ruler & Mat
  • Scissors
  • Sewer's Aid™ or Silicone Spray

Step One: Prepare Heat-Away

To make a scarf the size of our sample (7 1/2" x 43 1/2" flat), cut the 15" x 22" Heat-Away in half lengthwise (use pinking shears or a pinking rotary blade to avoid fraying). To make this into a circular scarf, overlap two 7 1/2" edges about 1/4" and straight stitch them together with Sulky Polyester Invisible Thread in the needle and bobbin.

Note: Sulky <u>Polyester</u> Invisible Thread is very heat tolerant and will not melt away like <u>nylon</u> invisible thread when the Heat-Away is disintegrated with a hot iron.

Step Two: Apply the Flat Braid or Wide Yarn

Starting at one of the overlapped seams and 1/4" in from the pinked edge, straight stitch down a flat decorative braid or cord lengthwise all the way around the edge of the Heat-Away until you get back to the starting point. Angle the braid 90 degrees and, without cutting it, stitch it down for about 3/4"; then, turn another 90 degrees and stitch down another long row. Don't worry about twists in the braid or uneven rows, they will add texture and interest to the finished scarf. If you are working with more than one continuous piece, simply overlap the cut ends and continue sewing.

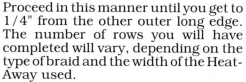

Proceed in this manner until you get to 1/4" from the other outer long edge. The number of rows you will have completed will vary, depending on the type of braid and the width of the Heat-Away used.

Note: If you plan to have more than 12 rows (like sample) you will need more than 30 yds. of flat yarn or braid.

Turn the Heat-Away 90 degrees, and continue adding the same braid in the same manner crossing previously stitched lengthwise braid. Angle the braid 90 degrees at the end of each row, stitch about 3/4", then turn another 90 degrees, and stitch another row back across the Heat-Away. Proceed in this manner until you get to 1/4" from the point of beginning.

Step Three: Apply the Faux-Weaver Yarn

Once rows of flat braid have been put all over the Heat-Away lengthwise and widthwise, change to a Sulky Decorative Thread in the needle and bobbin and add rows of straight stitching in between the rows of braid. You can make some of your own combinations of yarn/Sulky Sliver Thread by twisting them together using the SPIN-STER™ Twisting Tool (see Sources p. 137). You may also want to add other, thinner, decorative yarns as well. To attach these yarns, use a zig-zag stitch that is no wider than whatever you are attaching. If it is a lot wider, when the Heat-Away is removed, the thread will be loose. *Note: If you are going to add a thick yarn or braid, put it on last since it will be difficult to stitch back over it.*

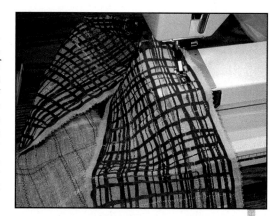

Step Four: Remove the Heat-Away

SET YOUR <u>DRY</u> IRON ON A COTTON SETTING. TEST YOUR HEAT SETTING ON A PRACTICE PIECE MADE FROM THE SAME MATERIALS THAT YOUR PROJECT SCARF IS MADE FROM. TO ACHIEVE SATISFACTORY RESULTS, SOME ENERGY SAVING IRONS MAY NEED TO BE TURNED TO A HIGHER TEMPERATURE.

Note: Make sure your iron is empty of ALL water. If any moisture gets on the Heat-Away, it could allow the chemical that causes Heat-Away to disintegrate to float into the yarns, threads, etc., making them disintegrate as well when a hot iron is applied.

A: When you have the Heat-Away filled with as many yarns, threads, etc. as you want, it is time to remove it. Cover your ironing surface with a pressing sheet or brown paper bag to protect it from the ash residue that the Heat-Away may leave behind when it is heated.

Turn your scarf inside out so the Heat-Away layer is up. Place the scarf (one layer at a time) on the ironing surface. To protect the bottom of your iron (unless it has a non-stick finish), place a press cloth over the Heat-Away. Press for about 15 seconds or until the Heat-Away turns to dark brown.

Continue pressing all the way around the scarf until all of the Heat-Away has turned dark brown. Place the scarf in a plastic bag and massage it gently to remove as much of the Heat-Away as possible. If there are any large pieces of Heat-Away left in the scarf, simply re-press it, being careful not to scorch the scarf with an iron that is too hot or left on the fabric too long!

B: To remove any little bits of Heat-Away that remain, brush them gently with an old toothbrush.

If the scarf is a little dusty, **but all the Heat-Away has been removed,** simply rinse it out in cool water and air dry. It may or may not need pressing when dry, depending on the braids and yarns that you have used.

WEAR IT WITH PRIDE AND ENJOY THE COMPLIMENTS!

Try expanding on this idea, perhaps by making your own fabric this way, then using it to make either a vest, an insert for a teddy, a collar or a lapel; or place it under a suit jacket or as an overlay where net or another sheer may have been the suggested fabric. Patti Lee models a scarf done in yarns and Sulky Threads. This yarn color is Rainforest.

ALTERNATE SOLVY (WATER SOLUBLE STABILIZER) METHOD

Instead of using Heat-Away as a foundation, the Solvy method is recommended when using yarns that have a low tolerance to heat.

1. If using ORIGINAL SULKY SOLVY, cut 3 to 4 pieces 8" x 45"; if using SULKY SUPER SOLVY, 2 layers should be enough. Fuse them together (use a press cloth to protect your iron unless it has a non-stick finish) by pressing with a **dry iron** at a cotton setting for only several seconds. Short ends will not have to be sewn together to form a circle because you can simply overlap them and press them together.

2. Follow directions for applying yarns on previous pages.

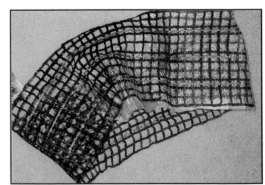

3. To remove the Solvy, submerge the project in warm water for 5 to 10 minutes. Because it is layered, you may want to rub the Solvy with your fingers to help dissolve it. Rinse well. If scarf seems stiff when it is dry, repeat Solvy removal process. If needed, press scarf with appropriate temperature for yarns used.

A bulky variation to making a Cowl Yarn Scarf

by Gina Butler
A Sulky Heat-Away™ Disintegrating Stabilizer Tip

You will need:
- ✔ **Sulky Heat-Away Stabilizer**
- ✔ Variety of Sulky Decorative Threads
- ✔ Bulky Yarns
- ✔ Thrube Yarn Feeder™

Instructions:

Before using Heat-Away, test yarns to be sure they are heat tolerant; if they are not, then use Super Solvy if yarns are water tolerant.

Follow basic instructions for Brenda Duncan's Faux Woven Scarf on p. 60, however, if you are using bulky yarns, the Thrube is a wonderful device to help place and feed them under the machine needle. After the "warp" and "weft" rows are done, stitch diagonally across the rows in both directions to create an "argyle" pattern.

If removing the Heat-Away Stabilizer causes the yarns to flatten, toss the scarf into the clothes dryer to refluff. This will also remove more of the excess stabilizer.

Hint: A quicker method of removing Heat-Away that doesn't flatten the yarns is to use a craft heat gun such as the "Heat-It" Craft Tool.

The finished size of the pictured Cowl Yarn Scarf is 12" wide x 24" in diameter, since it is stitched in a circle.

To make a stunning Sulky Sliver and Rayon vest like the one above that Joyce Drexler created, trace a vest pattern (Joyce used Sally Lampe's Long & Lean Vest Pattern) onto Super Solvy (2 layers fused together with a dry iron), adding an extra 3-5" all the way around the vest pattern to allow for "shrinkage" once Solvy has been stitched with all the yarn and braid. This was especially true on this vest since it was largely stitched on the bias. Once "fabric" is created, lay the vest pattern over it again and cut it out in the normal fashion.

Join shoulder seams (with right sides together) and overcast or serge them together.

Make a bias double-folded strip of fabric and stitch it around all the outside edges and armholes. Add a loop and button as a closure, if desired. Overlap side seams and add a strip of fabric down the side to stabilize and add interest. The added fabric piece may also be desirable to give you more "width" if your vest has "shrunk" in the stitching process. You could also construct traditionally, or serge it.

Fiber Jewelry
A *Heat-Away*™ *Disintegrating Stabilizer Project*

"Heat-Away is amazing! This is a product that stands up to embroidery with or without a hoop and is easily removed. Many years ago when I had a monogram shop, I tried a commercial product for making sew-on appliques, with less than desirable results. I am thrilled to be able to fully recommend Sulky Heat-Away to others for their sewing machine art. Don't you love it when a product does what it's supposed to do?" --- *Gina*

Gina Butler
of Oklahoma City, OK

For fourteen years, Gina owned and operated Gina's Stylized Stitching, a monogram shop in Oklahoma City where all of the work was done free-motion. The vast variety of jobs gave Gina an extensive training in the machine arts. She now teaches machine art classes in the Oklahoma City Bernina Stores.

She has taught classes for the National Machine Embellishment and Instructors Association (NMEIA), the California Association of Machine Embroiderers (CAME), Pro Show & Sewing Seminar, and various Bernina Dealers in Oklahoma, Texas and Missouri. Gina lives with her husband and 2 sons. The boys were raised in the monogram shop and began "drawing" with the sewing machine before they could reach the pedal.

Fiber Jewelry is sewn on Sulky Heat-Away Stabilizer using metallic braids and threads. The look is similar to a coarse bone lace or macrame, without the knots! Metallic Braids come in a wide variety of colors and weights and are very easy to work with. The strands can be attached to many jewelry findings. What will you make?

You will need:
✔ **Sulky Heat-Away Stabilizer**
✔ Sulky Metallic and
   Sliver Threads to match Braids
✔ Appropriate Jewelry Findings
✔ Metallic Braids
✔ German Hardwood Embroidery Hoop
✔ Sewing Machine set for Free-Motion
   Straight Stitch, no presser foot,
   lowered feed dogs

Instructions:

1. Wrap #16 metallic cord around a rigid piece of cardboard. You need 7 complete wraps around a 6" piece of cardboard for a key fob; or 10 wraps around a 4" cardboard for the watchband. Cut the cord on the side where you started wrapping. Use the folded side of the cut cord to attach to key ring with half hitch knots. Tie an odd number of strands - the odd one is split in two in the center of the row of knots.

2. Thread the machine needle and bobbin with Sulky Metallic Thread that closely matches the cording. Hoop the Heat-Away Stabilizer, catching the "unworking" strands (of watchband) in the hoop, leaving the "working" strands free. If you have strands only on one side, i.e. the key fob, tack the split ring to the stabilizer with free-motion jump stitches that will be removed after stitching is completed. TEST to make sure you are getting a balanced tension on your straight stitches, with no loops of thread on the underside of the work. The needle thread and the bobbin thread must meet evenly at the Heat-Away Stabilizer.

3. Draw up the bobbin thread and tie on. Clip excess thread tails. Begin shaping the strands by separating the center two strands and bringing them back together, crossing each other. Straight stitch down the left strand, into the cross and back up the right strand. Alternate left and right strands, stitching through the cord, into the next cross and again back up the other side. You don't have to follow the drawn pattern exactly - follow where the cords lead you! Just remember to secure the strands of cord at all crossings. A pattern should be duplicated on both sides of a watchband, so you may want to keep the design fairly simple. Since the key fob has strands only on one side, it is great fun to get wild with the design on it.

4. When your key fob is complete, straight stitch the strands side-by-side and trim the cord, leaving 1/2" to fray. To complete the watchband, you will need to compact the cords at the end and straight stitch them as tightly as possible. Sew on a bracelet clasp with jump stitches covering the clasp eyelet.

5. Cut the Heat-Away from around the sewn cords and split ring or watchband. Use a dry iron on cotton setting to disintegrate the Heat-Away. A quicker method is to use a craft Heat Gun. Place the corded piece in a shallow dish and watch as the stabilizer quickly turns to char. Lay the piece on a terry towel and press with your hands. The heat gun seems to be more thorough and doesn't flatten the work.

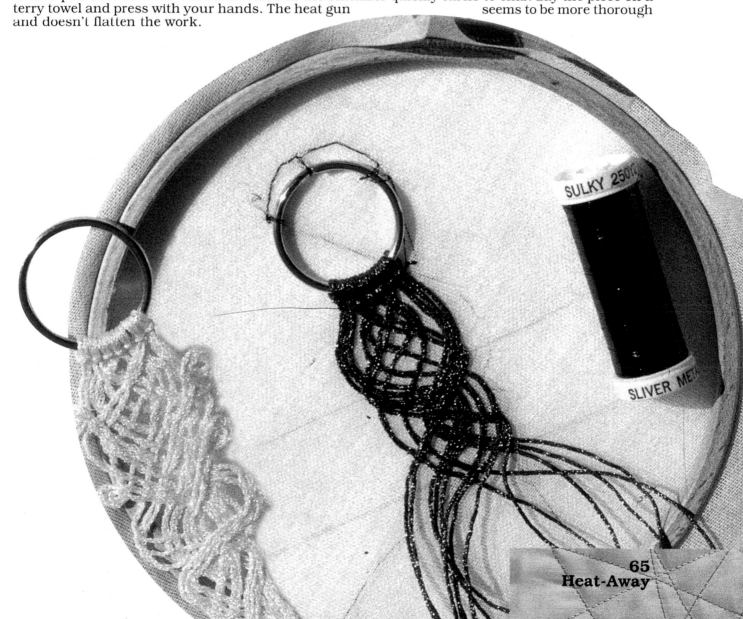

Pat Welch
Arvada, CO
A National Sulky
Educator

Pat has a B.S. from Iowa State University and an Advanced Degree from the Art Institute of Chicago. Pat is the President of Colorado Creations, as well as a partner in a Clothing Design Shop in Boulder, CO and an Adult Educator for Front Range Community College. Pat was the Educational Director for Bernina Sewing Chalets, a designer for a Western Wear Firm and taught High School and Jr. High School. She has been a National Sulky Educator since 1995. For fun, she organized a Fabric Lover's Tour of China in 1995.

"When the medium is yarn, small squares, or anything that needs a shape to build on, I use Heat-Away because it retains its shape as you build, then disappears with a hot iron, leaving light-as-air projects." --- Pat

Fringed Fabric
A Sulky Heat-Away Idea

Use this technique to make "fringed fabric" for a vest, jacket, inset, or home decorating project.

You will need:

✔ Zig-Zag Sewing Machine
✔ **Sulky Heat-Away Stabilizer**
✔ Sulky 40 wt. Rayon Threads
✔ Twin Needle - 3.0
✔ Coarse silk or other fabric that frays well. It took 36 three inch squares for 1 front of this small vest.

Instructions:

1. Cut 3 inch squares from the coarsely woven fabric.

2. To fringe, use a pin or tweezers to pull fabric threads out 1/4" around all four edges of each square.

3. Lay each square on a diagonal on the Heat-Away foundation with edges overlapping about 1/2"; leave little "peek-a-boo" boxes between each set of four. Pin in place.

4. Stitch with any decorative stitch through the centers of the squares in both directions. Pat used a 3.0 Twin Needle with an Heirloom Stitch and Sulky 40 wt. Rayon Thread in colors to blend with her chosen fabric.

5. Turn the fabric over so that the Heat-Away is on top. Put a brown paper bag under the garment to protect your ironing surface. Place a Teflon pressing sheet over the Heat-Away and press it with a hot, dry iron until it turns dark brown. **USE NO STEAM OR LIQUID OF ANY KIND.**

6. When the Heat-Away has all turned dark, place it in a plastic bag and crunch and massage it vigorously to remove the majority of the scorched stabilizer. Any remaining stabilizer can be removed by gently brushing it away with an old toothbrush. Rinse gently in cool water if your fabric permits.

Sheer Illusions

A Sulky Solvy™ Water Soluble Stabilizer Tip

Debbie Garbers & Janet O'Brien
Marietta, GA

Debbie Garbers and Janet O'Brien started In Cahoots , patterns and book company, as teachers and designers. Nationally recognized for their machine embellishment and wearable art, they have had garments in both the Fairfield Fashion Show and AQS Fashion Show, and vests in the '94 and '95 Sulky Challenge exhibits. They contributed to the book, *Embellishing Concepts in Sulky.*

The lower left section of the Sheer Illusions pattern is embellished with layers of sheer fabrics using a reverse applique technique. Solvy makes this technique easy and fun.

First, the stitching grid is traced right onto Solvy. Without Solvy it would be impossible to get accurate stitching lines. Even the lightest touch of a marking pen or chalk marker on sheer fabric makes it squirm and wiggle, producing lines that look like a snaking country lane. With the lines marked on Solvy, the lines are straight and they provide easy guides for stitching.

When the grid is completed, the Solvy is placed over several layers of sheer fabrics. The fabrics are smoothed out, and all the layers of sheer fabrics and Solvy are pinned in place. Solvy acts as a very lightweight stabilizer for stitching. When the stitching is finished, the fabric is placed in water where the Solvy dissolves completely, leaving the stitching and fabric smooth. There is no tugging and distorting of these delicate fabrics and no stray bits of stabilizer to remove.

Perfect Shark's Teeth

A Sulky Solvy™ Stabilizer Tip

Using Solvy when making Shark's Teeth with Clotilde's Perfect Pleater™:

Working on the wrong side of the fabric, apply a light application of spray stabilizer. Iron on 2 layers of Solvy (or one layer of Super Solvy). (I use my No-Stick Pressing Sheet on **top** of the Solvy to keep it from sticking to my iron.)

Then, peel off the No-Stick Sheet, and proceed to cut out and stitch the Shark's Teeth. This technique eliminates the need to tediously stitch individual pleats before shaping Shark's Teeth.

*"Eliminate crooked buttonholes, too. Draw a buttonhole ladder on a 2" wide strip of Solvy. Pin to shirt. Now stitch perfectly **parallel** buttonholes of identical length. Always cut with a buttonhole chisel, not a seam ripper."---* Clotilde

Clotilde

Clotilde, nationally recognized sewing authority, lecturer and author of <u>Sew Smart</u>, is Chairman of the Board of her mail-order sewing notions catalog company, Clotilde, Inc., established over 20 years ago. At the age of six, Clotilde picked up the needle and hasn't stopped sewing since. After graduation from Miami University of Ohio, she worked in the wardrobe department of 20th Century Fox Film Studio, where she learned valuable manufacturer's techniques of garment construction. She continued to learn designer tricks and techniques while sewing commercially for exclusive Beverly Hills boutiques.

Since the publication of her <u>Sew Smart</u> sewing book in 1977, she's crisscrossed the country giving seminars and in-service programs to Extension Agent groups, schools, fabric shops and trade show organizations. Clotilde has given lectures in countries around the world, including Canada, Australia and England. For two years, she was the host of her own cable TV program. She travels 30 weeks a year, teaching how to achieve the elusive look of expensive ready-to-wear at home.

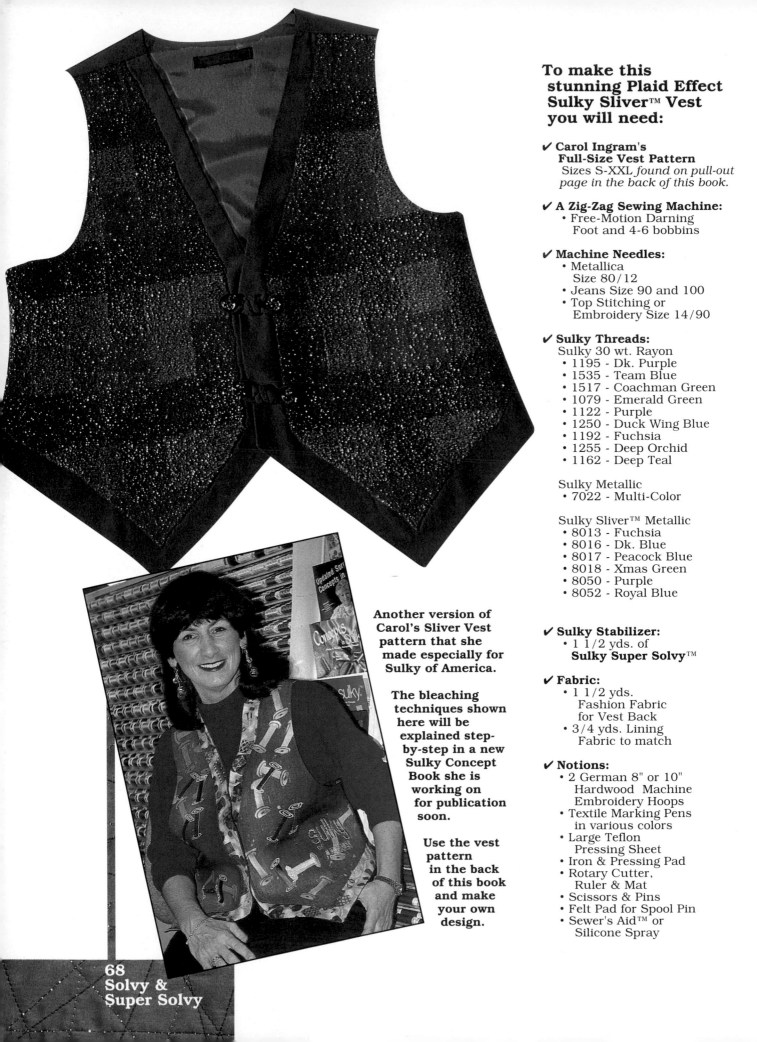

To make this stunning Plaid Effect Sulky Sliver™ Vest you will need:

✔ **Carol Ingram's Full-Size Vest Pattern**
Sizes S-XXL *found on pull-out page in the back of this book.*

✔ **A Zig-Zag Sewing Machine:**
• Free-Motion Darning Foot and 4-6 bobbins

✔ **Machine Needles:**
• Metallica Size 80/12
• Jeans Size 90 and 100
• Top Stitching or Embroidery Size 14/90

✔ **Sulky Threads:**
Sulky 30 wt. Rayon
• 1195 - Dk. Purple
• 1535 - Team Blue
• 1517 - Coachman Green
• 1079 - Emerald Green
• 1122 - Purple
• 1250 - Duck Wing Blue
• 1192 - Fuchsia
• 1255 - Deep Orchid
• 1162 - Deep Teal

Sulky Metallic
• 7022 - Multi-Color

Sulky Sliver™ Metallic
• 8013 - Fuchsia
• 8016 - Dk. Blue
• 8017 - Peacock Blue
• 8018 - Xmas Green
• 8050 - Purple
• 8052 - Royal Blue

✔ **Sulky Stabilizer:**
• 1 1/2 yds. of **Sulky Super Solvy™**

✔ **Fabric:**
• 1 1/2 yds. Fashion Fabric for Vest Back
• 3/4 yds. Lining Fabric to match

✔ **Notions:**
• 2 German 8" or 10" Hardwood Machine Embroidery Hoops
• Textile Marking Pens in various colors
• Large Teflon Pressing Sheet
• Iron & Pressing Pad
• Rotary Cutter, Ruler & Mat
• Scissors & Pins
• Felt Pad for Spool Pin
• Sewer's Aid™ or Silicone Spray

Another version of Carol's Sliver Vest pattern that she made especially for Sulky of America.

The bleaching techniques shown here will be explained step-by-step in a new Sulky Concept Book she is working on for publication soon.

Use the vest pattern in the back of this book and make your own design.

"Sliver into Color Vest"

A Sulky Super Solvy™ Project

*Presented by Joyce Drexler
on the PBS TV Program
"America Sews with Sue Hausmann"*

This exciting vest project shows the length to which you can go to express the bursting of color that can come from totally machine stitching Sulky Rayon, Sliver Metallic and Original Metallic Threads in jewel-tone colors over a foundation of Sulky Super Solvy to make the vest fabric. The finished piece emulates a silk plaid that would enhance any ensemble from day to evening wear.

*"This is a fun vest to do and is so satisfying to the true "free-motion" artist. It is not for the faint of heart or those without patience or endurance. I worked a total of 30 hours per vest, stopping to make notes, take pictures and ponder my plan of action. I did enjoy it and some may say 'she's nuts', but I enjoy a challenge.
My mind is racing at the possibilities for this technique! I used 2 to 2 1/2 180 yd. spools of each 30 wt. Rayon color and at least one spool of each of the 250 yd. Sliver colors, and 2 spools of Metallic, plus 5 spools of 30 wt. Rayon for bobbin thread."
--- Carol*

◀ **Use this vest pattern as a showcase for all your creative techniques.**

Vests on both pages were created by Carol Ingram and modeled by Julie Drexler (page 69) and Patti Lee (page 68).

Carol Ingram

of Lake Alfred, FL
Artist, Wearable
Textile Designer, Educator

Carol is an accomplished Artist in the Fine Arts field, including oil paintings, pastels and pencil drawings. She has studied art extensively at Community College and under private instructions from notable national instructors, and has a well developed concept of color and design. She has taught Elementary School Basic Drawing and the Color Wheel in a private school, along with giving private lessons. She has won many ribbons and awards for her works. Carol has sewn professionally for weddings, special occasions, and beauty pageants, which led to her knowledge of pattern drafting and fitting. She has sewn for a dance team of 30 girls, a clogging team of 11 girls and exclusively for several "Teen Miss" Beauty Pageant contestants. Her forty-year background in sewing has provided her with special insight into designing and creating wearable art which has helped her fulfill her desire to be a textile and machine artist. She presently teaches techniques in textile art at Fabric Warehouse in Lakeland, FL and other surrounding shops. Carol won first prize in the 1996 Wearable Art Category of the Annual Sulky Challenge --- her "Tiger" project is featured in this book. Look for more of Carol's work in an upcoming Sulky Book to be published in 1998.

Step One:

For each vest front, layer together two 20" x 25" (or a size suitable for your chosen vest pattern) pieces of Sulky Super Solvy and fuse them together by applying a Teflon pressing sheet and a hot, dry iron for several seconds.

Place the vest front pattern piece in the center of the Super Solvy. Use a colored fabric textile marker in a base color to draw around the outside edge of the pattern, adding about 3/4" all the way around to allow for shrinkage due to the amount of free-motion fill-in stitching that follows.

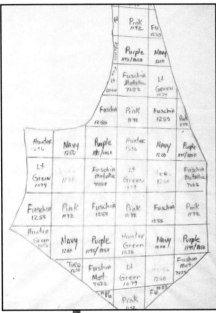

Step Two:

Using a quilter's ruler and the same textile marker, draw a 2" grid over the entire pattern.

Step Three:

Decision making time! At this point, you need to have a plan of action for your colored grid. Carol was inspired by a plaid fabric she had used for a silk ribbon pillow she had made some time ago. Following the design in the fabric, she drew a 2" grid and indicated the colors with the same color marker in that square along with the Sulky Thread color number and type for easy reference at the sewing machine. This makes for a wonderful colored map to stitch by and it will aid you a great deal if you have to lay the project aside and days later return to work on it. This way you will know exactly where you left off and where the correct thread colors should be stitched.

Step Four:

Set up your sewing machine for free-motion:
 1. Lower the feed dogs.
 2. Attach a free-motion darning foot.
 3. Insert a new size 14/90 embroidery needle.
 4. Thread the top and bobbin with Sulky 30 wt. Deep Teal #1162.
 5. Select the straight stitch.
 6. Tension adjustment: You do not need to adjust your tension while using the straight stitch. However, as soon as you begin using the zig-zag and/or Sliver thread, you will need to drop your top tension dramatically.

Hooping:

Working on a flat surface, lay the Solvy vest front over the outer ring of the hoop. Insert the inner ring and press down with the heel of your hand. Once the hoop is as tight as possible, thump the center; it should have a "drum" sound with no looseness in the center. Because you will rehoop and change thread colors and types many times, at some point in the rehooping process, because of the bulkiness of the stitched areas, hooping may become difficult. Using a high-quality German hardwood hoop with a solid brass screw closure allows you to tighten the hoop with a screwdriver. Don't be timid with Super Solvy, it can take it! Stitch three times over all the grid lines on each pattern front to create stay-stitching for further embroidering. To prevent perforating the Super Solvy, do not stitch over and over the exact line of stitching, but rather right next to each other.

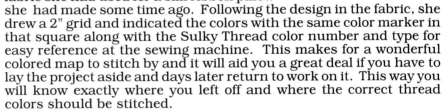

Step Five:

Using a circular motion with the hoop, completely cover the entire grid pattern with large circles; make sure each circle comes around and connects with the last circle, joining all the circles over the entire grid pattern. This stitching serves as a base for the application of the Sulky Rayon, Metallic and Sliver Threads. Coverage does not have to be particularly dense, but do not leave any large, sparsely stitched areas.

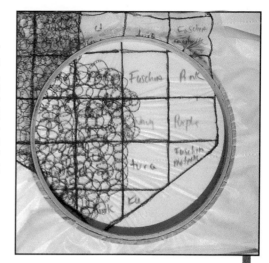

Step Six:

Thread your machine with one Rayon 30 wt. color and one Sliver of the same color through the same size 100/16 needle. Fill your bobbin with the same 30 wt. Rayon. The handling of two threads, either Sliver or Metallic with 30 wt. Rayon was a dream with relatively no breakage or shredding using the Thread Pro™. Thread each thread independently through their own tension on the Viking #1+, and then both through the eye of the needle, avoiding the final thread guide just above the needle.

It is of utmost importance to hoop and rehoop the Super Solvy very tautly to prevent stitches from drawing and shrinking the grid. Choose your starting place in one of the center squares of the grid.

Using a large width zig-zag stitch, begin in the corner of the square and zig-zag up and down to sparsely cover the entire square. Change your hand motion to a side-to-side fill-in stitch and, starting at the top (or bottom) of the square, move the hoop slowly back and forth, making a line of fill-in stitching from one edge of the square to the other and then back again until the entire square has been filled smoothly. The side-to-side motion elongates the stitch and completely shows off the flat, shiny Sliver Thread the best. When you have finished one square on the right front piece, repeat the procedure on the left front piece in the same mirrored square.

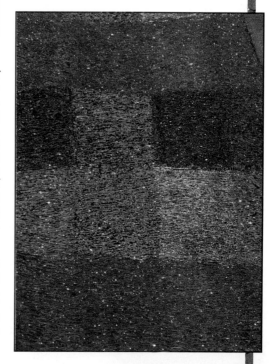

Change thread colors and begin stitching the square next to the completed one; do the same thing in this square, making sure your zig-zag motion from left and right connects and goes slightly into the previously stitched square. This connecting of squares also helps to hold the finished project together. Continue this until both sides of the vest are entirely covered. *(In my case, 20 hours later!)*

At several stopping points between hooping, use your original vest pattern piece that you drew around in Step 1, to check sizing and shrinkage. Make any necessary adjustments such as enlarging the grid area or adding squares so it fits the vest pattern before the shrinkage becomes a major problem. You should expect some minimal drawing up, but not anything that you can't overcome if checked periodically.

If the vest piece is not handled properly and kept tautly in the hoop, it could become warped out of shape.

Tip: Get organized and save time ...
Organize thread colors beside your machine. Prewind bobbins. Use two separate hoops. Utilize the largest needle that accommodates the job. Although Super Solvy responds exceedingly well to continual needle punctures and stretching in the hoop, if you have a mishap that makes a hole in the Solvy, it can be easily patched by ironing a small piece of Solvy (larger than the hole) to the underneath with an iron and teflon pressing sheet. If the stitching should pull away and cause a hole to develop, you can cut a piece of Solvy (slightly larger than the hole) from the edge of your working piece, slide it under the hole and continue stitching over the patch.

Step Seven:
It's pure heaven when you finish your last color! Trim away the excess Super Solvy from around the edges of each piece. Place the entire finished pieces in a sink of cold, clear water and dissolve away the Super Solvy. Rinse thoroughly. Roll the pieces in a terry towel, block them, and allow them to dry.

Step Eight:
While the pieces are drying, construct the back of the vest and the outside facings or bias edge for around the vest fronts. Use an iron-on interfacing inside the facing that acts as a trim for the vest front. To add a professional finish to the inside of the vest, finish the inside edge of the facing with a serger stitch using a matching Sulky 30 wt. thread color. Finished facing on the sample vest was 1 1/4" on the outside and 1 3/4" on the inside.

Step Nine:
Once the front stitched panels are dry, lay them on top of the front facing and attach them with a blind hem stitch using a 30 wt. Sulky Rayon Thread that matches the base color. Sew to back and add ties if desired.

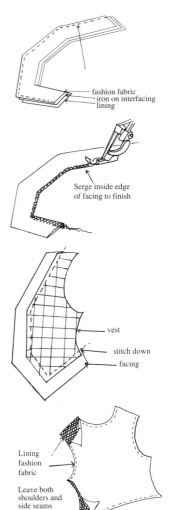

fashion fabric
iron on interfacing
lining

Serge inside edge of facing to finish

vest

stitch down
facing

Lining
fashion fabric

Leave both shoulders and side seams open for turning

Using the same techniques as in the original Sliver into Color Vest, Carol made this beautiful Cut-work style Sliver Vest for Joyce to wear on the TV Show, "America Sews with Sue Hausmann". Instead of filling in all the squares, she left every other one empty. The pattern she used for this vest was the LONG AND LEAN by Sally Lampe, with techniques shown in this book. You could make a 1" grid if you preferred a smaller cutwork look.

Cozy Cardinal

A Sulky Super Solvy™ Stabilizer Applique Tip

Linda Bealmer
Mapleton, IL

Linda's business started out by creating designs for shirts to sell at a craft mall. When people started asking for the patterns, she decided it was time to write them out and share them. She has been marketing "Sew Mini Pieces" pattern line since 1994.

"The background fabric on the "Cozy Cardinal" is a loosely woven 100% cotton. After it is prewashed, all the sizing comes out of it, making it too soft for machine applique. To make it nice and crisp and much easier to machine applique without distorting the fabric, I dissolve 1/2 yard of Super Solvy in 8 oz. of water and paint it onto the fabric with a brush. After it dries, it holds its shape beautifully as I machine applique, but it isn't too stiff to wear because all of the Super Solvy washes out when I launder it. I also use liquid Super Solvy for the basket lining. Since the basket is actually woven using bias tubes, when I attach the tubes to the lining, it's a little difficult to maintain the shape of the basket because the lining is so soft. Stabilizing the lining with liquid Super Solvy reinforces the fabric with sizing, making it so much easier to maintain its shape. So many times it's those little things we do that no one sees that make all the difference in the outcome of a project." --- Linda

Fabulous Fabric

A Sulky Solvy™ Stabilizer Tip

Virgie Fisher
Fairfield Designer
Newalla, OK

"This was the second Fairfield design I had created and I wanted to represent Fairfield's sponsors in this knock-out two-piece ensemble presentation which took me three months to create. Sulky provided thread for the design, and gave me unlimited freedom to further develop my 'Fabulous Fabric' technique using Sulky Solvy as the base product.

To create the fabric, I sandwich Sulky Decorative Threads between several layers of Solvy which allows me to separate the colors for strategic placement. Then I place the layers of Solvy and threads on a teflon pressing sheet, spray them with a very fine mist of water, and cover them with a second teflon pressing sheet. I press all sheets together, let the project cool and dry, peel away the pressing sheets, place the project in a hoop and free-motion embroider it with small circular stitches, making sure stitches overlap. After the entire surface is worked, I rinse with warm water until all Solvy is removed. When project is dry, I place it on a sheet of Solvy, hoop and add couching, embroidery and other embellishing techniques. I repeat this process as many times as necessary to complete the project. I add jewels, beads, sequins and charms for the finishing touches to 'Fabulous Fabric'." --- Virgie

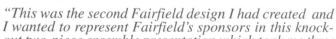

To Make this Vest Joyce used:

✔ **Timeless Treasures/ Hi Fashion Fabric:**
  • Sky - Viewpoint #16
    Color: Ice
  • Woods & Mountains -
    Viewpoint #23
    Color: Ice
  • Waterfall Rocks -
    Viewpoint #15
    Color: Navy
  • Lining and Binding -
    Tonga #39
    Color: Night
  • Muslin Foundation
    pieces cut to the
    size of your vest
    pattern

✔ **Sulky Threads:
  40 wt. Rayon**
  • 1180 - Mountains
  • 1046 - Grasses/Trees
  • 1131 - Trees
  • 1071 - Tree Accents

✔ **Sulky Sliver Metallic**
  • 8040 - Snow /Clouds

✔ **Sulky Polyester
  Invisible Thread
  for the Bobbin**

✔ **Zig-Zag Sewing Machine:**
  • Free-Motion Darning Foot
  • Edge Foot, Open-toe Applique Foot
  • Machine Embroidery Needle 14/90

✔ **Sulky Stabilizers:
  Super Solvy™ & Tear-Easy™**

✔ **Notions:**
  • 3-4 yds. Steam-A-Seam 2™
    Double-Sided Fusible Web
  • Ironing Surface and Steam Iron
  • Sharp Pointed Scissors
  • 8" or 10" German Hardwood
    Machine Embroidery Hoop
  • Quilters Straight Pins
  • Fine-line, Permanent-Ink Marker

"Embroidered Fabric Print Landscape Vest"

Using Super Solvy™ as a Stitching Pattern

by Joyce Drexler
As shown on the PBS TV Program
"America Sews with Sue Hausmann" Program AM402

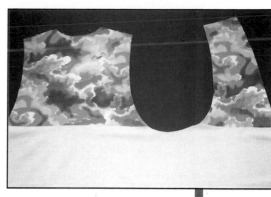

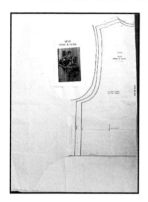

Step One: Prepare the Muslin Foundation Vest Pieces.

To make one continuous piece of muslin from your vest pattern, eliminate the side seams by overlapping the sides of the pattern pieces, matching the stitching lines; then cut muslin as one piece. In this example, the "Long & Lean" vest pattern by Sally Lampe was used.

Step Two: Prepare the Fabric Landscape Applique Pieces.

1. Cut a piece of the sky fabric that will cover the top half to 2/3 of your vest from the shoulders down. *Be sure clouds are billowing UP, not down.* Following package directions, apply Steam-A-Seam 2, fusible web, to the wrong side of the sky fabric. Fuse to Muslin Foundation.

2. Apply fusible web to the wrong side of the mountain, land areas, birch trees and foreground rocks & bushes. Cut out the design along rock tops. Cut off the tops of the stand of trees at mountain top level. The trunks of the trees should be cut right along the line leaving no background other than low hills. The foreground rocks need to be cut in different groups and levels. Also, cut out several of the bushes.

Step Three: Arrange and Fuse Down the Mountains, Land and Lake areas, and Birch Trees over the Sky Fabric.

Make this a fun adventure! Don't be afraid to play with your fabric pieces. By having the double-stick fusible web on them you can reposition them over and over before fusing them in place. (You can achieve the same effect with Sulky KK 2000 Temporary Spray Adhesive and any paper-backed fusible web.) Having the birch trees on both fronts of your vest is a pleasing look. Start on the fronts and work your way around the vest. If you have chosen a vest design that overlaps in the front, make the flow of the design continuous. Create more interest in your design by arranging and stacking the mountains at different levels to make various elevations. Try to have only one or two mountain waterfalls per vest section.

Note that the lake water must stay level with the horizon, so be sure it is positioned correctly before fusing it in place.

Place the dark foreground rocks and waterfalls last. Lay one large section with the pool-like area for the contour of the foreground. Place the bluish bushes at the bottom edge. Add more rocks cut to various sizes to cover the area as needed. Position rocks at different levels, not just as they are on the printed fabric. Fuse.

Step Four:
Set up your Machine for Free-Motion Embroidery.

1. Lower or cover the feed dogs.
2. Attach the free-motion darning foot or quilting foot.
3. Insert a new Embroidery Needle size 14/90.
4. Thread the top with Opalescent Sulky Sliver #8040. Use Sulky Clear Invisible Polyester Thread in the bobbin. Select a straight stitch.
5. Loosen top tension to almost zero or until no bobbin thread is pulled to the top of the work.
6. Place a section of the sky fabric in a 10" wooden machine embroidery hoop or, do not use a hoop if you are experienced at free-motion and prefer more access to the design.

Step Five:
Begin embroidering over the Landscape Print.

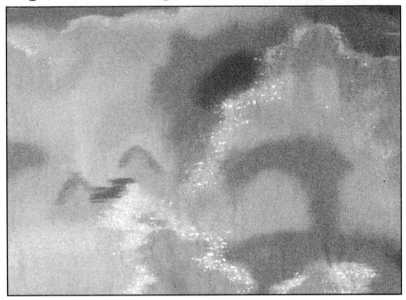

1. Sky - Using a straight stitch and side-stitch outlining motion, add a light, open outline around some of the cloud shapes. Keep the Sky horizontal at all times and simply ease around the shapes, feathering into them with a side-stitch motion.

2. Mountain Tops - Continue using the Sulky Opalescent Sliver and add a little glitz to the snowy mountain tops.

3. Land, Rocks and Water Add Opalescent Sliver to the snow on the land areas, foreground rocks, waterfalls and lakes.

Step Six:
Continue Embellishing with Sulky 30 wt. or 40 wt. Rayon Thread.

1.Thread up with Sulky Rayon Med. Taupe #1180.   Select a straight stitch and free-motion embroider parts of the mountains.

2. Change to Teal Green #1046, and use a straight stitch to free-motion embroider the distant trees and grasses.

Step Seven:
Satin Stitch over the Tree Trunks and Limbs on the Fabric Print.

1. Place two layers of Tear-Easy Stabilizer under the tree area. Thread up with Cloister Brown #1131. Use Sulky Invisible thread in the bobbin. Select a wide satin stitch. Attach an open-toe applique foot. With feed dogs up, satin stitch over the tree trunks.

2. Continue satin stitching up into the limbs of the tree, reducing the width of the stitch as necessary to just cover all of the limbs on the print.

3. Build up the satin stitching to your satisfaction on all of the stands of trees throughout your vest.

Step Eight: Make a "Fusible" Super Solvy Tree Limb Pattern.

1. Secure Super Solvy in a 10" German Hardwood Machine Embroidery Hoop. To make tracing easier, lay the hooped Super Solvy on the remaining fabric piece where limbs are intact and use a black, fine-line, permanent-ink marker to trace the top branches that were cut off at mountain level. Trace only the most prominent limbs. You will add finer branches on your own when you are stitching.

2. Pop the Solvy out of the hoop and pin it into position, lining up branches so they match with the satin stitching you did over the fabric print. Place a steam iron just above the Solvy and shoot it with steam. *This will make the Solvy a fusible,* **and it will adhere to the fabric** when it dries, making it much easier to hoop and rehoop to free-motion embroider on the tiny limbs. You can also make Solvy adhere to fabric by spraying it with KK-2000 and finger-pressing it over tree trunks.

3. Using the same width setting you ended with on the top of the limbs on the previous page, continue satin stitching on the Solvy Pattern, reducing the width setting as needed until you are finally using only a straight stitch. Switch to free-motion, hoop the tree-tops, and add delicate straight stitch branches. Thread up with Off-White #1071 and stitch the accents on the trees.

4. Gently pull off as much of the Tear-Easy Stabilizer as you can, one layer at a time from the back of the trees. Next, gently pull off as much of the Super Solvy from the front as possible. Thoroughly rinse the remaining Solvy from the vest; be sure no stabilizer remains in or on the vest as it will make the vest stiff.

5. Allow vest to dry, then press it well. Finish vest construction following vest pattern instructions. Top stitch along all edges of the vest using your edge foot and Sulky 30 wt. Rayon Thread in a color that coordinates with your vest.

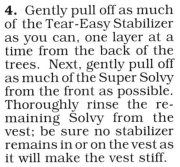

Beaded Puff Pin & Earrings

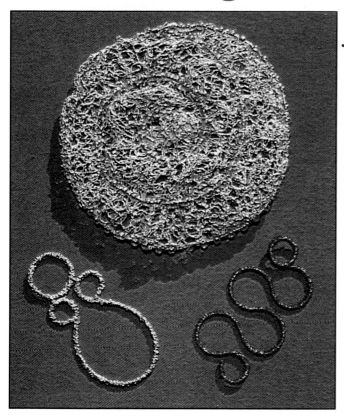

Using Solvy as a Foundation for Stitching

by Neda Starr
A National Sulky Educator from Vallejo, CA

"I chose Sulky Solvy because it can be rinsed away completely; any other stabilizer might have left little bits behind that would have spoiled the lace." --- *Neda*

You will need:

✔ **Sulky Solvy Stabilizer**
✔ Sulky Threads:
   Metallic Multi-Color Silver/Light Copper/Electric Blue #7028
   Sulky Clear Invisible Polyester Monofilament
✔ Seed beads
✔ Florist Wire that will fit through beads
✔ Aleene's Thick Designer Tacky Glue
✔ Sewing Machine Needles:
   Size 70/10 for invisible thread
   Size 90/14 for metallic thread
✔ German Hardwood Embroidery Hoop
✔ Extra-Fine, Permanent-Ink Marker
✔ Pin-Back

Instructions:

1. Set machine for straight stitch free-motion embroidery by lowering the feed dogs and removing the presser foot. Fill one bobbin, half-full, with Sulky Clear Polyester Invisible Thread. **(Wind the bobbin <u>very slowly</u> when using invisible thread.)** Wind a second bobbin with Sulky Metallic #7028. Tension on the machine should be balanced.

2. Put 3 layers of Sulky Solvy tightly in the hoop. Trace the design and the grid lines from the pullout pattern sheet onto the Solvy with a fine-line, permanent-ink marker.

3. Using Sulky Invisible Thread in the needle and the bobbin, free-motion straight stitch the outside edge of the design, and then the grid lines.

4. Change to Sulky Metallic #7028 in both the needle and the bobbin, and stitch overlapping "e's" over the entire design to create "Spun Lace". (See technique on p. 71.)

5. Bend a tiny crimp in one end of the wire and thread some beads onto the other end. Place the crimped end of the wire in the center of the design and cover it with small zig-zag stitches. Push up a bead, then continue zig-zag stitching over the wire. Follow the spiral design, pushing up a bead about every 1/4" - 3/8". Do not completely cover the wire with stitches; they will be closer together after the gathering. When spiral is complete, fasten off threads, but leave a wire tail about an inch long.

6. Remove from hoop, dissolve and rinse away Solvy. Allow to dry.

7. To gather, push the lace up on the wire a little at a time and ease fullness along the wire towards the center, causing the lace to puff up.

8. To finish: crimp the end of the wire and cut off excess; bend the crimped end to the back and apply a drop of glue; glue a pin-back to the wrong side, and it's ready to wear.

Sulky Thread Sculptured Rose Bud Pin

by Gina Butler

A *Super Solvy*™ Water Soluble Stabilizer Idea

"Super Solvy and Sulky thread make my flower jewelry come to life. Solvy is strong, yet easy to remove. By intentionally leaving some of the Solvy in the piece, the embroidery maintains its dimension during wear. Sulky thread gives flowers that 'dew kissed' appearance that makes them look freshly picked from the flower garden." --- Gina

Thread Sculpture is the art of creating fabric from machine embroidery threads. Pieces can be formed into any shape imagined. This is a very good technique for those who are new to the machine arts. Wonderful results can easily be achieved using only a straight stitch. For flower patterns, look to seed catalogs and books on gardening. Of course, those of you with "green thumbs" can "pick" patterns from your own gardens.

You will need:

- ✔ **Sulky Super Solvy**
- ✔ Water Soluble Pen
- ✔ Sulky 40 wt. Rayon Thread in your choice of colors
- ✔ German Hardwood Embroidery Hoop
- ✔ Bar-Pin
- ✔ E-6000 Fabric Glue
- ✔ Patterns on Pullout Pattern

To design your flowers, cut petal shapes from paper or muslin to experiment with before beginning to stitch. Another fun source for flower patterns are ready-made silk flowers. It's very beneficial to "sacrifice" a silk flower to see what shapes are necessary for the results you desire.

Instructions:

1. Hoop 2 to 3 layers of Sulky Super Solvy. With a water soluble pen, draw the outline of the shape to be filled in. Because both sides of your sculpted fabric may be seen at once, thread the needle and the bobbin with Sulky 40 wt. Rayon Thread. For realistic effects, use a darker shade in either the needle or the bobbin.

2. Lower the feed dogs, remove the presser foot, and set the machine for straight stitch. Outline the shape to set the border. To create the base, circle stitch the entire shape, being sure to let the circles overlap each other, forming "links". Don't worry if you can see

small openings of light among the circles, but do try to stitch fairly evenly without large gaps.

3. Now you're ready to stitch the flower texture. Straight stitch over the circle stitches "in the direction of growth". You will actually create a grain, stitched from the center of the flower and fanned outwards to the petal edge. Leaving "controlled" gaps in the work can act as "darts" to help when you're ready to shape the flower.

4. When the petals and leaves are as solid as you would like them, remove the project from the hoop and cut away the excess Super Solvy. Dip embroidered piece in water to **partially** dissolve the remaining Super Solvy. The Flower can now be "sculpted" to desired shape. Bend the petals for a more natural appearance. If too much Super Solvy was removed causing it to be floppy, you may add a liquid Solvy Stabilizer (see page 9 for instructions). While pieces are damp, roll and pinch bud at base. Set leaf at base and wrap calyx around both pieces. A number of things can be used as a shaping/drying rack: i.e., a thread cone, a plastic top from a spray can, or you can create exactly the needed shape by making a ring from foil. When dry, secure with sewing machine straight stitches. Glue bar-pin to back and enjoy!

Credit: This method is fully described in Yvonne Perez-Collins' book entitled **SOFT GARDENS - Make Flowers with Your Sewing Machine**, published by Chilton Books. Additional methods of thread sculpture and patterns to use are: "Flutterbys" - Gail Roulet, Chickasha, OK - a pattern featuring monarch butterflies; and "Butterfly - Antique Irish Crochet on the Sewing Machine" by Mary Ray Osmus, Benecia, CA.

Embroidered Toddler's Terry Bib
Easy as 1-2-3!

A Solvy™ Water Soluble Stabilizer and Tear-Easy™ or Sticky™ Stabilizer Project

"Solvy is the ideal topper for terry towels when machine embroidering or monogramming. It holds down the loops of the towel and allows the thread to be delivered in a smooth, even flow so coverage is excellent. When the embroidery is completed, it tears and/or washes away without a trace. It's magic! Nothing works better." --- Nancy

Nancy Cone
from
Port Charlotte, FL

Nancy has sewn for most of her life, making clothes for herself and her family. She now is a Sewing Machine Sales Representative and Instructor at Charlotte County Sewing Center in Port Charlotte, FL.

You will need:
✔ **Sulky Solvy and Sulky Tear-Easy or Sulky Sticky Stabilizers**
✔ Sulky 40 wt. Rayon Thread in your choice of colors
✔ Sulky Bobbin Thread and Sulky 40 wt. Rayon Thread that will match the towel
✔ Machine with computerized Embroidery capabilities, Nancy used the Bernina DECO 600
✔ Serger - optional
✔ Embroidery Design Card
✔ Knit Ribbing (3 1/2" x 12") (cotton is softest)
✔ T-Towel (11" x 17")
✔ Water Soluble Pen

There are endless possible designs for children's Bibs. Choose designs that suit the sex of the child. Then pick ribbing that best matches or coordinates with the design. Every mother will appreciate how this bib covers the child while teething or eating. It makes a most appreciated and inexpensive Baby Shower gift! And it will be used!

Instructions:
1. Prepare the Towel.
Fold one end down horizontally 5"; pin to hold. Fold the towel in half lengthwise to find the center of the horizontal fold; mark it with a water soluble pen. Unfold towel lengthwise. Make 3 marks, each 2 3/4" away from the center mark, to the left, to the right, and down. Make the neck opening by cutting a 5 1/2" wide by 2 3/4" deep semicircle along the folded edge.

2. Prepare and Attach Ribbing.
Use a 1/4" seam allowance and an overcast stretch stitch (or use a serger) to sew together the short ends of the 3 1/2" x 12" ribbing. Fold in half lengthwise, wrong sides together, making the band 1 3/4". Divide the band into halves horizontally by holding the sewn seam and putting a pin into both ends. Fold to divide into quarters; mark with pins.

Repeat for the towel opening. Match the 4 pins in the ribbing with the 4 pins in the towel, placing the seam of the ribbing at the center back of the towel. Using an overcast stretch stitch by machine or serger, stitch together, stretching ribbing between pins to fit towel opening. Top stitch rib edge down.

3. Embroider the Towel.
Into the DECO 600 embroidery hoop, layer 2 pieces of Tear-Easy (spray with KK-2000 to make it into a "sticky" type stabilizer or use one piece of Sulky Sticky) cut larger than the hoop, followed by the towel and a piece of Solvy. Note: if using a velour towel that might sustain marks if the top hoop is used, hold each layer in place with KK 2000 and omit the top ring of the hoop. Insert the hoop in the machine and embroider. Remove the bottom stabilizer first by tearing it away.

Then gently tear the Solvy away. If any remains, spray with water and gently rub with a paper towel.

Suzy Seed
of Houston, Texas
A National
Sulky Educator

Suzy has worked in the sewing industry for over 20 years; 14 in retail sales, 4 in wholesale, and several as a cutter and sewer for a custom designer. She attended Texas Womans University. She has taught everything from beginning sewing, fitting, color and line to Machine Arts.

No Pins! Faux Paper Piecing

A Super Solvy™ & KK 2000 Quilting Tip

Paper Piecing Design by Eileen's Design Studio

You will need:
✔ **Sulky Super Solvy Stabilizer**
✔ Quilting Thread
✔ Extra-fine, Permanent-Ink Black Marker or Sulky Iron-On Transfer Pen
✔ Fabric Scraps
✔ Sulky KK 2000 Temp. Spray Adhesive
✔ *See Pullout Pattern*

Joyce's Tip:
To make tracing easier on smaller projects, hoop the Super Solvy in an embroidery hoop to hold it taut or spray the pattern with Sulky KK-2000, then lay the Super Solvy over it.

Instructions:
1. Spray Sulky KK 2000 onto Super Solvy, then lay another layer on top of it, or iron 2 layers of Super Solvy together using no steam and a press cloth.

Then choose one of the three following tracing methods:

A. Spray your chosen design with KK-2000. Place the 2 layers of Super Solvy over the design and trace it with an extra-fine, permanent-ink marker. The KK 2000 holds it in place.

B. For quick multiples, trace the design once onto a plain piece of paper using a Sulky Iron-on Transfer Pen, then heat transfer it onto the Super Solvy.

C. Use a rubber stamp paper-piecing design to make multiples of your design. Test the stamp pad ink to be sure it will not bleed into your fabric.

2. Starting with #1, spray the wrong side of the chosen fabric with KK 2000. Begin piecing as you would with paper, placing the right side of the #2 fabric to the right side of the #1 piece as indicated on the pattern. Press as you go with a DRY iron. (If your iron does not have a non-stick surface, use a press cloth.)

3. Trim away the excess fabric and Super Solvy 1/4" from the outside stitching lines (along the dotted lines on the pattern); save Solvy scraps to start delicate seams or small projects (see below). Using Super Solvy instead of paper is so much faster and easier because you avoid the tedious and time-consuming tearing and picking out of paper; you can actually leave the Super Solvy underneath until it is seamed in. You don't have to remove it until later with the first washing. Or, you can press the Super Solvy with a dry iron until it is brittle and it will pull away easily.

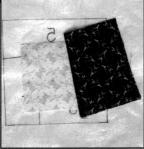

Knit Edge

by Suzy Seed

A Super Solvy™ Water Soluble Stabilizer Tip

When starting a seam on nylon tricot or a knit of any kind, you can start your stitches on a doubled piece of Super Solvy so the edge doesn't knot up. Use a 3.0 width and a 1.0 length right on the edge for a sheer, small seam. One stitch falls in the fabric and one stitch is over the edge. This would also work on sheer fabric for a small finished edge.

Gathering with Solvy

A Solvy™ Water Soluble Stabilizer Tip

Patti Jo Larson
of Sheyenne, ND

Patti Jo Larson is a regular on the PBS TV program, "America Sews with Sue Hausmann". As a traveling Education Consultant for Viking, she loves inspiring others to be creative with their sewing skills. Specializing in heirloom sewing and working with French sewing experts, Martha Pullen and Kathy McMakin, she has brought Traveling Schools of Art Fashion across the United States.

You will need:
✔ **Sulky Solvy**
✔ Ruffler Foot or Gathering Foot

"The Ruffler and Gathering feet are two "must have" accessories for your sewing machine. I love how fast and precise either one can make nice and even gathers or pleats on all sorts of fabric. By using Solvy, these accessories can now successfully gather even fine lace edging so that it looks nicer and fuller than that which you can buy." --- Patti Jo

Instructions:

1. Strips of Solvy sewn along the edge of lace allow the Ruffler or Gathering foot to turn flat yardage into ruffled trim. Both accessories work best when the "to be gathered" fabric has a seam allowance because the Gathering Foot needs to ride on both sets of feed teeth, and the Ruffler's pleater slide must catch into more than air. Solvy provides the "seam allowance" so that you can run the gather stitching right along the edge of the most delicate lace.

2. French lace edging for heirloom sewing: While French lace has gathering threads built into the header, pulling them to distribute the gathers by hand can be very tedious. Recently I made my daughter, Joanna's, Baptism gown with a full circle skirt and 10 yards of 1 1/2" wide lace-edging to be gathered.

It would have taken hours to pull up that much twisted, tangled lace into uneven gathers. You just hope the header thread you are pulling doesn't break. But strips of Solvy and the Gathering Foot turned this lace into a beautiful ruffle in minutes...a real time and stress saver. Instead of laboring tediously for hours, I actually held Joanna on my lap and stitched effortlessly, using only one hand, while she watched intently. The lace formed beautiful, even gathers almost by itself, thanks to Solvy and the Gathering Foot.

Serger Lace
by Patsy Shields

Super Solvy™ as a Serger Aid

"Sulky Super Solvy is the perfect stabilizer for this project. It removes easily, doesn't affect the needle, and can be folded or layered as many times as need be to give you the effect you want."
----- Patsy

You will need:
✔ **Sulky Super Solvy**   ✔ Serger
✔ 3 spools of Sulky 30 wt. Rayon Thread in your color choice to match or contrast with your fabric/garment choice.

Instructions:
1. Thread the left needle and upper and lower loopers with your color choice. Use a balanced, wide three-thread stitch with a stitch length of 2.
2. Cut Super Solvy a few inches longer than you need the lace to be, and about 6" to 8" wide.
3. Fold one end of Super Solvy up about 1", serge on the fold.
4. Open out the fold and refold just enough to serge another row of stitching on the Super Solvy, catching into the edge of the previous row of serging. Repeat until you have the lace as wide as you like.
5. Attach the lace to the fabric/garment either with the sewing machine or the serger, then remove the Super Solvy by rinsing or washing the project.

It's in the Bag
Pendant or Pouch

A Sulky Super Solvy™
Water Soluble Stabilizer Project

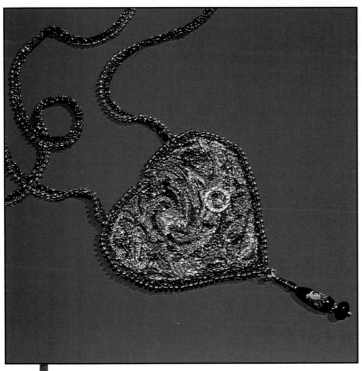

Mary Lu Stark
A National Sulky Educator from Albuquerque, NM

Mary Lu received a Bachelor's degree in Fine Art with a Major in Studio Art from the University of New Mexico. She was a Quilt Shop Owner from 1978 to 1985. She has been the Director of numerous Quilt and Art-To-Wear Seminars, most notably, NEW MEXICO QUILT FIESTA 1981 and 1989 and FASHION FLIGHTS OF FANCY 1990 with Ann Rae Roberts. Mary Lu teaches wearable art classes and workshops for guilds, shops, and private groups on a free-lance basis; she specializes in pieced clothing, jackets and belts with emphasis on fabric manipulation, embellishment, texture and pattern originality. She has been a National Sulky Educator since 1994.

She is part owner (with her daughter, Lara) of Pink Haus Studio in Telluride, Colorado where they show and sell their bead work and other wearables.

You will need:
- ✔ **Sulky Super Solvy Stabilizer**
- ✔ **Sulky Tear-Easy Stabilizer**
- ✔ Sulky Rayon Thread in desired background color
- ✔ Sulky Metallic and Sliver Thread
  Step-by-Step Model used:
  - 7012 - Lavendar
  - 7015 - Jade Green
  - 7052 - Peacock Green
  - 7020 - Gold/Turq./Pink
  - 8050 - Purple
  - 8001 - Silver
- ✔ Sulky Bobbin Thread (White or Black)
- ✔ Sulky Invisible Thread
- ✔ 6" German Hardwood Embroidery Hoop
- ✔ Metallica 12/80 and Embroidery Needle 70 or 75/11 and 14/90
- ✔ 1 1/2 yds. Crossed-Lock Beads
- ✔ 1 1/2 yds. Cord (Satin Cord, Rat Tail, or make your own)
- ✔ Beads: Just a few - check to be sure hole is large enough to allow a size 70-75 needle to clear.
- ✔ Small piece of Fleece and Ultra Suede for backing
- ✔ Tweezers for bead work
- ✔ Beading Foot and/or Cording Foot
- ✔ Pattern found on Pullout Pattern Sheet

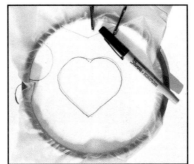

Instructions:

1. Decide on shape of design (on pullout pattern sheet) and trace shape onto an 8" square of Super Solvy.

2. Set up machine for free motion. Select a 5" or 6" square of fabric with colors or lines that appeal to you to help you get started. If you don't need this help, use a piece of fabric in any solid color because the fabric will not show when the piece is finished.

3. Sandwich fabric between one 8" square of Super Solvy on the bottom and Super Solvy with traced pattern on top in a machine embroidery hoop. Using Sulky 40 wt. Rayon Thread on top, Sulky Bobbin Thread in the bobbin and a size 14/90 embroidery needle, free-motion straight stitch around outer edge of pattern to contain the shape.

4. Change to 3.0 width zig-zag and start filling in the background with a side-to-side movement. Remember, fabric is just a "starter" -- don't try to copy the print -- just fill in some shapes. Then start filling in the blanks using different colors of Sulky Metallic and Sliver threads; carry each color in small amounts throughout the pattern, building up the colors until the over-all effect is pleasing to you. This is a small piece, so it won't take long to fill it in.

5. Now the fun begins with the beads. Just a few will be needed for the final touch. Insert a size 75 embroidery needle; upper tension remains lowered as in free-motion set-up.

6. With a Sulky Metallic (Mary Lu's favorite for this is multi-color 7020 because it seems to blend in with most colors and enhance the work as it progresses) or Invisible Thread in the needle and Sulky Invisible in the bobbin, use a free-motion straight stitch to apply beads one at a time. Place beads at least 3/8" from the edge all the way around so as not to interfere with the bead foot later when adding the crossed lock beads and cord to edge of pendant.

7. To attach beads, fasten on thread and, with needle in up position, use tweezers to place a bead, hole up, next to thread. Take one stitch in center of bead, then one stitch on side of bead as close to bead as possible. This stitch should pull bead over on its side. If it does not, use tweezers to roll it over. Stitch to next bead site and repeat the process to attach another bead, continuing in this manner until desired number of beads have been attached.

8. Remove your "jewel" from the hoop and trim away the Super Solvy and excess fabric. Cut two or three layers of fleece slightly smaller than pendant and place under pendant. Cut rectangle or square of Ultra Suede about 1/2" larger all around than the pendant, and place them under pendant and fleece. Raise feed dogs, attach regular sewing foot, and use normal sewing tension. Use a Sulky Metallic or Invisible thread that will blend in with other colors to baste edges of pendant to Ultra Suede with a narrow zig-zag stitch. If a more weighted pendant is desired, insert weights or coins inside piece between fleece layers before closing the edges. Trim Ultra Suede to edge of pendant.

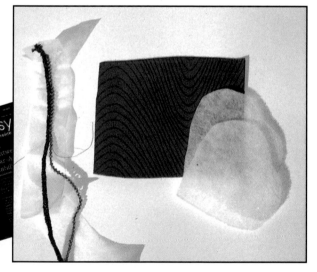

9. To suspend the pendant, cut satin cord or metallic braid the desired length. Put Metallic Thread on both top and bobbin. Place a strip of Sulky Tear-Easy under the cord to stabilize it while stitching crossed-lock beads onto it. Use a 4.0 to 4.5mm width zig-zag stitch and 2.5 to 3.0 length. (Test stitch length and width on your machine so that stitches fall between beads and around cord.) Apply crossed-lock beads to edge of neck cord. After stitching is completed, carefully remove the Tear-Easy strip. Insert each end of beaded neck cord into upper edge of pendant between front and back.

10. At center front of heart pendant, insert one end of remaining cord and one end of crossed-lock beads between front and back of pendant. Using a wide zig-zag or blanket stitch, attach cord and crossed-lock beads between front and back of pendant, then simultaneously around edge of pendant starting and ending at center front. Trim away excess cord and beads and push ends into pendant at starting point of stitching. Fashion a beaded dangle or other accent and attach it to the bottom of the pendant.

TO MAKE AN AMULET POUCH:

1. Select one of the rectangular shapes and add another layer of Ultra Suede to the back during the completion stage. Leave an opening at the top between the two layers of Ultra-Suede to form the pouch. Sew crossed-lock beads across the top of the back piece first, then continue around the edge of the pouch, up and around the neck cord, down to the starting point on upper side of the pouch.

2. For closure, make loop of seed beads (use some of the crossed-lock beads for this purpose) and attach by hand to the center back of pouch. String a short dangle of seed beads with a larger bead at the end to pull through the loop and attach it to the center front of pouch.

TO MAKE A BROOCH:

After applying cord and crossed-lock beads around edge, simply sew or glue pin-back on the back side of the brooch. *Sign your work --- be proud!*

Embroidered Woven Xmas Pillow Tip

*Presented by Joyce Drexler
on the PBS TV Show
"Sew Creative" with Donna Wilder.
Step-by-step weaving techniques found
in the Embroidery Concepts in
Sulky Book 900B-10.*

Using Solvy as a Topper to hold down unwanted fabric fibers.

Joyce's Tip:

When we further developed a weaving technique (by Lois Ericson as featured in "Threads" Magazine with their permission) for the Sulky "Sew Exciting" Seminar Vest, we discovered that by using a low count cotton fabric with a raw edge, the fibers wanted to poke up into the decorative stitching. To eliminate this problem, we layered Solvy over the woven piece and then stitched. To keep the Solvy in place without pins, we lightly sprayed the top of the woven piece with KK 2000, then finger-pressed the Solvy layer over it. The Solvy kept the fibers out of the way so our decorative stitching with Sulky 30 wt. Rayon and Sulky Metallic Sliver™ Threads looked fantastic!

Stabilizing for Fagoting by Machine

by Carol Laflin Ahles

Using Super Solvy as a Sewing Aid for Heirloom Sewing

You will need:
- ✔ **Sulky Super Solvy**
- ✔ Straight lace 5/8" to 3/4" wide
- ✔ Spray Starch

Tip:
To prepare to join lace to fabric by fagoting, fuse lace and fabric temporarily in the desired position by lightly spray-starching the wrong side of the lace and fabric; lay them in place over Super Solvy, cover with a press cloth, and press with a dry iron. Use the same technique when joining lace to lace.

"Using Super Solvy is a real time saver for my lace techniques. In classes, students often expressed their frustration at having to fuse and press two layers of regular Solvy together to get enough strength and body for these techniques. Super Solvy is the perfect weight so it eliminates the need to fuse layers together." --- Carol

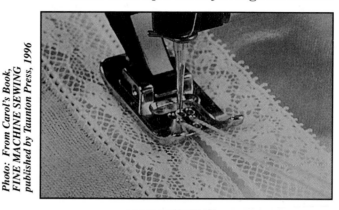

Photo: From Carol's Book, FINE MACHINE SEWING published by Taunton Press, 1996

Peggy Forbes
Pfaff Educational Consultant

Peggy Forbes has been a sewing enthusiast since she was a small girl standing at her aunt's side "supervising" the construction of her 1st grade wardrobe. Years later, Peggy was bitten by the "quilting bug" which led to a new career at a local Pfaff dealer's store, teaching quilting and wearable art. Peggy is an award winning quilter having taken top honors at state and county fairs.

Lace Heart Ornaments
Using Solvy or Super Solvy as a foundation for Computerized Embroidery

You will need:
- ✔ 2 **Super Solvy** pieces 9" x 9" (or 4 Solvy pieces 9" x 9")
- ✔ Pfaff Fantasy Choice Card with Lace Medallions Design
- ✔ Pfaff Creative 7570 and Creative Fantasy Unit
- ✔ 120 Hoop or Pfaff Big Hoop
- ✔ Embroidery Foot
- ✔ Heirloom Cotton Thread
- ✔ Ribbon ✔ Size 80 Machine Needle
- ✔ Tapestry Needle

Instructions:

1. Hoop 2 layers of Super Solvy or 4 layers of regular Solvy. With Pfaff's Big Hoop, 6 ornaments per hooping can be stitched.

2. Thread the machine both top and bobbin with heirloom cotton thread of your choice.

3. Select lace embroidery design. In this project, the Pfaff Fantasy Choice Program #115669 (lace heart) was used.

4. With right cursor arrow, enter move screen.

5. Move design to upper right corner with right cursor arrow and key #9.

6. Stitch design with balanced tension.

7. When design is finished, select move screen and move design just far enough away so that you can stitch the design again without overlapping. This will let you stitch several designs without rehooping.

8. Stitch design. Repeat #'s 4 through 8 until hoop is filled with embroidered designs.

9. Soak ornaments in warm water only until Solvy is dissolved but not completely rinsed away so that ornaments will retain body shape. Allow to air dry.

10. Insert a ribbon through each ornament with a tapestry needle. Tie off and hang.

Serger Fagoting

A Super Solvy™ Water Soluble Stabilizer Tip

Kathy McMakin

of Huntsville, Alabama
Contributing Writer and
Construction Editor
for Sew Beautiful magazine

Kathy is a graduate of Samford University and a gifted educator. She teaches classes in heirloom sewing by machine and serger in cities across America and internationally. She has written three books and has appeared as a guest instructor in several sewing videos. Kathy is married and has two teen-age children.

You will need:

✔ **Sulky Super Solvy Stabilizer 2 pieces, slightly longer than lace pieces**
✔ Sulky Rayon Threads: 2 spools of 30 weight #1001 Bright White
✔ 2 Pieces of 1" Lace - desired length
✔ Either Pearl Cotton Sulky 30 wt. or 40 wt. thread in your color choice

Instructions:

1. Cut 2 pieces of lace to the desired length.

2. Cut 2 pieces of Super Solvy about 1 1/2" wide and slightly longer than the length of the lace pieces. Fuse Super Solvy together by pressing with a dry, hot iron for several seconds.

3. Baste or glue (with KK 2000) the lace strips onto the Super Solvy strip about 3/16" apart.

4. Set the serger for a 6 mm cover stitch. Thread both needles with Sulky 30 wt. #1001 Bright White and thread either Pearl Cotton, 30 wt. or 40 wt. Sulky thread in the cover stitch (lower) looper.

5. Run the lace/Super Solvy Strip through the serger allowing each of the serger needles to stitch through the lace headings.

6. Cut away the excess Super Solvy from the outside of the stitching. Soak the lace/Super Solvy strip to remove the remaining Super Solvy. Press well. Use the strip to decorate and embellish heirloom clothing.

Sulky Solvy Tip *by Jim Suzio:*

To reduce the effects of "hoop burn" (the marks made on some fabrics by the heat generated by the friction of the inner hoop being inserted into the outer hoop) add a piece of Solvy on top of your fabric, then place in the hoop as normal. This eliminates damage to the fabric, and the transparent Solvy allows you to easily see your placement marks; AND, it dissolves with a misting of water! No bulk is added to your embroidery and the fabric remains unmarked.

Continuous Line Quilting

A Sulky Tear-Easy™ Quilting Idea

*As presented by Joyce Drexler
on the PBS TV Program -
"Kaye's Quilting Friends" with Kaye Wood*

"Formal Garden"

You will need:

✔ **Sulky Tear-Easy Stabilizer**
✔ Continuous Line™ Quilting
   Design *by Hari Walner
   (Pattern found on the pullout
   pattern sheet in back of book)*
✔ Sulky Rayon Thread:
   30 weight: #1149 Deep Ecru
✔ 10" Square of Top Fabric
✔ 10" Square of Batting
✔ 10" Square of Backing Fabric
✔ Matching Sewing Thread
✔ Coordinating Fabric for
   borders & backing on your
   pillow or quilt blocks
✔ Copier Machine

Instructions: Using a dark, fine-tip marker, trace onto a plain 8 1/2" x 11" sheet of paper, the Continuous Line Quilting Design found on the pullout pattern at the back of this book. Place it face down in a copier machine. Using double-sided tape, tape a sheet of 8 1/2" x 11" Tear-Easy Stabilizer onto a piece of paper and manually feed it into the copier to copy the design onto the Tear-Easy, giving you a perfect lightweight tear-away pattern to stitch over (ideal for repeated quilt blocks). Pin Tear-Easy design onto your layered "quilt sandwich". Set your straight stitch length to 2.8 or 3.0 and, using an open-toed applique foot or even-feed foot and your color choice of Sulky 30 wt. thread, stitch over the lines on the pattern. Tear away the stabilizer carefully when stitching is complete. Tear-Easy is perfect since it is lightweight and won't tear out your stitching. Use it for copier machine-made paper-piecing designs too!

Concentrated Cording

A Tear-Easy™ Stabilizer Tip

by Pauline Richards

You will need:

✔ **Sulky Tear-Easy**
✔ Braid foot
✔ Sulky Clear Invisible Polyester
   Monofilament Thread
✔ Decorative Braid

Instructions:

1. Copy an embellishment pattern onto Tear-Easy.
2. Mirror image the embellishment design onto the right side of your garment or fabric.
3. Position the embellishment guides on the right side of your garment or fabric.
4. Attach a braid foot on your machine and thread it with braid. Set your machine for a straight stitch.
5. Use conventional thread in the bobbin, and Sulky clear or smoke polyester monofilament through the top of the machine.
6. Position the presser foot directly over the embellishment guide lines and begin stitching.
7. Lift and reposition the presser foot as necessary to insure accuracy as the trim is stitched into place.
8. Tear the stabilizer away and close the seams or complete the garment according to the guide sheet directions.

Foundation Piecing
A Kaliedoscope Wallhanging
A Tear-Easy™ Quilt Piecing Project

Sue S. Moats
A National Sulky Educator

Sue is an educator at "G" Street Fabrics and a Chautauqua Artist at Glen Echo National Park, MD, where she enjoys teaching young students through the quilting process. Sue retired after 27 years of teaching math and computer classes to pursue her love of quilting. She has been teaching sewing and quilting classes for about five years. Sue is a National Sulky Educator, and likes to travel to teach their "Sew Exciting" Seminars. Sue loves to "play" with different fabrics to create new textures using metallic and variegated threads or yarns. Her quilted wall hangings have been in numerous quilt shows, and some of her garments have been juried into prestigious fashion shows. Two of her garments will be in <u>Artistic Apparel</u>, a Singer Reference book being published by Cowles Publishing Co.

"Foundation Piecing and Scrap-Look Quilts are two popular trends with quilters. Combining them is a very easy process using Sulky Tear-Easy Stabilizer and a Sulky Iron-On Transfer Pen. While Foundation Piecing began as an effective way to produce miniature quilt blocks, many other quilters are using Foundation Piecing to produce more accurate blocks of any size. Since Foundation Piecing is stitched from the <u>back</u> of the block on the foundation with the fabric <u>underneath</u>, it is a good idea to start with a simple block and work up to the more difficult designs as one becomes more familiar with the technique." --- Sue

The Kaleidoscope wall hanging was an easy project based on a Mosaic Art Design by Mark Pickens. Sue and Mark participated in a joint show in which Sue interpreted some of his designs in fabric. A portion of the design was enlarged with a color photocopier to make the interpretation easier to do.

You will need:
✔ **Sulky Tear-Easy Stabilizer**
✔ Sulky Iron-On Transfer Pen
✔ Sulky 40 wt. Rayon Thread #2241 (multi-color)
✔ Sulky Smoke Invisible Polyester Monofilament Thread
✔ Kaufman Kona Cottons in various colors
✔ Striped Denim
✔ Lightweight Fleece for filler
✔ Calico backing
✔ 4.0 Twin Needle
✔ Rotary Cutter, Mat and Quilt Ruler
✔ Teflon Pressing Sheet

The Kaleidoscope Block Design to be used is on the pullout pattern sheet; it is adapted from Block #64, page 79 of the book <u>101 Foundation-Pieced Quilt Blocks</u>, by Linda Causee with her permission. The original design has a seam through the center of two main fabric pieces, so Sue has redrawn it to move that seam to a place where an actual seam exists.

Instructions:

1. Use a Sulky Black Iron-On Transfer Pen and a quilt ruler to trace the Kaleidoscope block design (from pullout pattern sheet) onto light-weight white paper. **Be sure to add 1/4" seam allowances** as needed on all four sides and wherever units of the block(s) must be joined to complete them. Some resources include the seam allowance, but the <u>101 Foundation-Pieced Quilt Blocks</u> book does not.

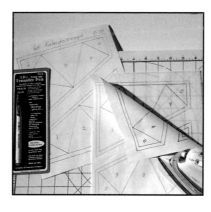

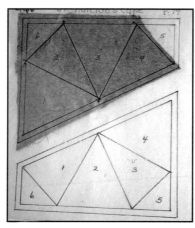

2. Cut Sulky Tear-Easy Stabilizer into the number of pieces, in the size needed to construct your blocks. Place the traced block on the Sulky Tear-Easy and <u>press</u> with a dry iron set on cotton until the image has transferred to the stabilizer. Lift a corner of the transfer paper to be sure the design has transferred before removing the paper. Continue transferring to the other Tear-Easy squares until all the blocks are complete. If necessary, re-ink the transfer image. If you can use a pressing iron, you will be able to get much clearer and many more images from the original transfer.

(I was able to get 12 transfers from one good "inking" this way --- Sue)

4. Continue to complete each block unit and then join them together as indicated by the block design. Leave the Sulky Tear-Easy foundation on all blocks until they are completed and joined into the quilt top, and the borders have been added. This helps to stabilize the units during construction and to eliminate stretching along the seam lines where bias fabric may have been used.

5. When the quilt top is complete, select a compatible backing and batting, fleece or flannel as desired. Make your "quilt sandwich" and decide what quilting design you want to use. The Kaleidoscope wall hanging was quilted along the seams in the design with a 4.0 twin-needle with Sulky 40 wt. Rayon #2241 (multi-color) in both needles. Sulky Smoke Invisible was used in the bobbin as well as later, in the single needle, to stitch in the ditch on both sides of the narrow black border.

Hint: If you want to make a garment, such as a vest, jacket or coat with foundation piecing, an alternative method would be to use the Sulky Iron-On Transfer Pen to copy the block designs and transfer them to prewashed cotton flannel for the foundation, then proceed as in the directions.

Some of the common Foundation Piecing mistakes to avoid are:
- *Omitting 1/4" seam allowances.*
- *Using the wrong side of the fabric.*
- *Fabric pieces too small or positioned incorrectly.*

3. Now you are ready to begin the fun of constructing the blocks. From your scrap bag, select the first fabric which will fit the space. Position the fabric in front of the foundation block and hold them up to the light to be sure the fabric will cover both the space and the seam allowance. Pin in place. Then select the second fabric and test it to be sure it will cover the next space. Pin in position, flip over the block and stitch from the back on the line between the two sections. Turn over the block, flip over the 2nd fabric, finger press and continue with the next fabric.

Chain Stitching by Machine
A Sulky Tear-Easy™ Stabilizer Quilting Tip

Eleanor Burns

Eleanor Burns has written and published more than fifty books that sell at a rate of 6,500 per week. She appears on Pulbic Television with her show, "QUILT IN A DAY". She developed her simple sewing and quilting methods while a busy mother of two boys.

" I hate that puckered-up look! With Sulky Tear-Easy Stabilizer, I just get smo-oo-oth stitches!!"
--- Eleanor

You will need:
✔ **Sulky Tear-Easy**
✔ Sulky 30 wt. thread in your color choice to match your pearl cotton
✔ Pearl Cotton
✔ Washable Marker
✔ A background fabric square
Blocks that include chain stitching from Quilt Block Party Series Six
APPLIQUE IN A DAY
- not included in this book

Instructions:

1. With a washable marker, trace a line onto the background square. Pin Sulky Tear-Easy Stabilizer behind the square.
2. Cut a piece of pearl cotton twice as long plus several inches more than the line. Match Sulky 30 wt. rayon thread color to pearl cotton.
3. Set machine stitch length at 2 for small, tight, outline stitch, or 3 for a long, open stitch.
4. Place center of the pearl cotton on one end of the line. Stitch back and forth over pearl cotton. Use "needle down" position if your machine has one.
5. Pull pearl cotton across presser foot and hold the ends taut. Take three machine stitches. Stop with needle in fabric.
6. Criss-cross pearl cotton in front of the needle. Stitch over pearl cotton, and take three machine stitches.
7. Stop with the needle in the fabric, and criss-cross pearl cotton again.
8. Continue to stitch and criss-cross until line is covered. Backstitch.
9. Perforate stabilizer by removing thread from needle, and sewing on "chain stitch" with a very small stitch.
10. Gently pull stabilizer away.

• Distlefink

• Evening Blooms

• Spring Flowers

• Grape Wreath

Elegant Evening Clutch

A Sulky Stiffy™ Crisp, Firm Tear-Away Stabilizer Project

"I prefer to use Sulky Stiffy because I only have to use one layer to stabilize most fabrics. For a project like my evening bag, Stiffy also gives the project the body it needs without using additional interfacings. Because Stiffy is so firm, I only need one layer when I am embroidering. I team it with Sulky Sticky when embroidering on T-shirts and sweatshirts. When I remove the stabilizers, my work is always smooth and unpuckered." — Tom

Tom Kohl
of Winter Haven, FL
Designer, Educator, Retailer

Tom and his family own and operate AK Sew & Serge in Winter Haven, FL. He has also published a line of wearable art patterns under the company name of "Nooooo Problem Patterns". His fascination with sewing began many years ago when he would "play" with his mother's sewing machine. "Playing" turned into a creative outlet, and then a business. Tom still teaches many classes at the store. Over the past several years, Tom has also taught at several Sewing Machine Company conventions and appeared on several television sewing programs. He has taken classes from nationally known sewing professionals, and he is a certified Kaye Wood instructor.

You will need:
✔ **Sulky Stiffy Stabilizer**
✔ Sulky Sliver Thread in a color that coordinates with your satin choice
✔ Sulky Bobbin Thread
✔ Sewing Thread to match satin
✔ Metallica Needle size 14/90
✔ Metallica Twin Needle 3.0 14/90
✔ 1/3 Yd. Bridal Satin
✔ 1/3 Yard Fusible Fleece
✔ Pintuck Foot
✔ Edge/Joining Foot
✔ Washable Marker

Instructions:

1. Straighten the cut edges of your bridal satin fabric using a mat, ruler and rotary cutter. Cut a 2" piece off one selvage edge (the short side), and put this piece aside.

Cut 2 pieces of bridal satin (one for the lining and one for the outside) and one piece of fusible fleece 11" wide and 21" long.

2. Set up your sewing machine for embroidery. Use a Metallica needle, Sulky Sliver thread on top and Sulky Bobbin Thread in the bobbin. From one of your monogram or lettering cards, choose the initial (or initials) you wish to put on the clutch. Fold one 11" x 21" piece of satin in half, lengthwise, to find the center.

Hoop the satin as close to the selvage of the fabric as you can so the excess lies to the back of the sewing machine. Align the center fold line with the markings on the hoop. Place the hoop on the embroidery unit. Cut an 11" x 20" piece of Sulky Stiffy and place it under the hoop. Line up the needle with the center fold line so your monogram will be centered. (If your machine does not automatically position the needle to show the center of the design, check your placement with the template for the hoop you are using.) Sew your letter or monogram. Leave the Sulky Stiffy behind the outer fabric to give the purse more stability.

3. Take the fabric out of the hoop, fold it in half lengthwise with the Stiffy Stabilizer on the inside, then fold it in half widthwise. Place folded sides on the bottom and right. Place a long quilting ruler at the upper right hand corner and cut the top edge (not the side with the fold) at a 45° angle. Then cut the piece in half along the widthwise fold. Fuse the lining piece of satin to the fusible fleece.

4. Insert a Metallica twin needle. Thread the top of the machine with two spools of the same color of Sulky Sliver; be sure to place each spool on its own vertical spool pin. Keep the Sulky Bobbin thread in the bobbin.

Place monogrammed piece right side up with the monogram facing upward away from you. With a washable marker, beginning with one of the bottom corners, draw a line at a 45° angle. Put a pintuck or a satin stitch foot on your machine. Sew a row of straight stitching on your marked line. Putting that row of stitching on the outside edge of the sewing foot, sew another row. Continue in this manner until you have stitched a total of 8 rows. Press your fabric if required.

5. Thread your machine with regular sewing thread and insert a single needle. Put right sides of lining and purse together, and straight stitch around all of the sides except the straight bottom edge. Turn your purse right side out and press.

With the 2" strip of satin cut earlier, bind the straight raw edge by folding the satin strip in half the long way; put the raw edges to the short straight side of the lining and straight stitch them together at 1/4". Then fold the strip around to the right side of the purse and edge stitch it using your edge foot.

6. Sew the side seams to finish the purse. Divide the fabric into thirds, marking the lines with a washable marker. Keeping right sides together, fold the straight bottom edge on the first line up to the second line. Stitch the side seams very close to the edge of the fabric. Turn right side out and press. Place Velcro or a snap on the flap to hold shut, and you are finished.

"Buttonhole or Blanket Machine Stitched Fusible Fabric Applique"

A Totally Stable™ Iron-on Tear-Away Stabilizer Project

Elaine Waldschmitt
Johnston, Iowa

A quilter for almost 20 years, Elaine has won numerous awards for her quilts including "Viewers Choice" at a local show and "Honorable Mention" for her Farmers Daughter Quilt in the 1995 American Quilters Society Show in Paducah, KY. In 1995, Elaine started designing for her own pattern company, THE QUILTED CLOSET.

Applique Designs featured in Elaine's Pattern, *FISH LAKE TEES.* One Size Fits All.

"Fusible Web Applique is so easy and fun to do, but many fabrics (especially T-Shirt knits) require a stabilizer to prevent puckering and shifting. I have found that even if the fabric being fused onto is stable, Totally Stable will help my sewing machine create more even and accurate decorative stitches on the applique. On my 'Fish Lake' Denim Shirt, I ironed Totally Stable behind the denim prior to fusing the applique. This helped eliminate shifting and stretching during fusing and allowed for beautiful buttonhole stitching around the fused fabric applique. Sulky Totally Stable was a breeze to remove compared to other 'Tear-Aways' I have used. Any remaining stabilizer left my project soft and comfortable to wear." --- Elaine.

Joyce's Tip:
Sulky 30 wt. Rayon Decorative Thread is perfect for Machine Buttonhole Applique. For an even heavier stitched look, use two 30 wt. threads through one 16/100 needle. Reduce top tension slightly.

"This quick and easy blanket-stitched applique project was done on a ready-to-wear sweater, but could be done on a sweatshirt or other garment of your choice. With the array of jungle prints available in fabric stores, the possibilities are endless.

Don't be limited to only using a knit fabric. This technique could be easily adapted to a denim jacket or shirt. If you truly enjoy making garments, ignore the ready-to-wear suggestion that will be embraced by those of us who lean more towards embellishing.

The sweater used in the sample was an extra large. Some of us are more 'ample' than others, so adjust the applique design elements to fit the garment size you choose, adding more or using less, whatever is appropriate for the look you are striving towards." --- Patti

"Tiger in the Jungle" Appliqued Sweater

A Sulky Totally Stable Stabilizer Project
by Patti Lee

Presented by Joyce Drexler on the PBS TV Program "Sew Creative" with Donna Wilder.

"Totally Stable is my removable stabilizer of choice when working on sweater knits which tend to distort so easily. It irons on simply, and in as many layers as you need to control the knit." --- Patti

Patti Lee
of Englewood, FL

Patti has been involved with Speed Stitch and Sulky of America on both a part-time and/or volunteer basis since both companies were formed. She is currently Consumer Relations Director for Sulky of America. She was a National Instructor for Speed Stitch, and an active participant in all nine of their annual S.M.A.R.T. Events. She has also worked in retail sewing machine and fabric stores. In addition to being a contributor to several Sulky Concept Books, she also acts as Joyce Drexler's Assistant and has her own creative business, Lee Designs.

1. Apply Fusible Web to the back of Leaf and Branch Fabrics

Using Steam-A-Seam 2, double-sided fusible web, remove the printed release sheet and place the web, sticky-side down, on pull-out pattern for applique. Trace all the long leaves with a permanent marker onto the unprinted release sheet. Peel up and hand press onto the green fabric you have chosen to be the long leaves. Cut out pieces. You can reposition Steam-A-Seam 2 again and again to make the most efficient use of your fabric. (The same results can be accomplished with Sulky KK 2000 Temporary Spray Adhesive and any paper-backed fusible web.) Repeat step one for large leaves and branches.

2. Cut Animal Print and Netting

The Animal! Choose the animal print (lion, tiger, bear, etc.) that you wish to feature on the garment. Since the nylon net will actually be placed on top of the tiger when it is appliqued to the garment, cut out all three at once... animal, Steam-A-Seam 2 and nylon net. Remove the printed release sheet from Steam-A-Seam 2 and place the sticky side against the back of the tiger. Peel away the plain release sheet and place a piece of nylon net (with metallic sparkles) against the sticky side. Cut out all 3 following the outline of the tiger (leave no seam allowance).

3. Prepare Garment

To simplify the applique process enormously, cut open the side seams of your pullover garment to create a relatively flat surface on which to work. Apply a moderately hot iron (NO STEAM) for several seconds to press two layers of Sulky Totally Stable to the wrong side of the front of the garment in all areas that you will be stitching. If Totally Stable works loose after lots of handling, just repress to restick it. You can save and reuse any excess Totally Stable which you tear away after you've finished stitching.

4. Placement

Peel the 2nd release sheet from the branch pieces. Position branches using the placement diagram as a guide, or get creative and design your own placement which may be dictated by the size and type of garment you are using. Use more or less branches to accomplish the look you want for your unique original piece of wearable art. *Remember: With Steam-A-Seam 2 or Sulky KK 2000, you can reposition the pieces again and again up until the time you fuse them in place with an iron.*

If desired, remove the release sheet from all the pieces at this time and play with the layout until you're satisfied that this underlayer of branches is where you want it to be. The other pieces can be replaced onto a release sheet to save until you're ready to use them. Before fusing, try on your garment to be sure you are pleased with your layout and placement of pieces. Once satisfied, steam press them in place.

5. Thread Machine and set up for Blanket-Stitch Applique

Thread the bobbin with Sulky Invisible Thread (clear for light fabrics or smoke for darker fabrics). Because Sulky Invisible Thread is a lightweight **polyester** monofilament, it has a much greater tolerance to heat than nylon monofilament; perfect for projects requiring fusing or pressing with a hot iron. Thread the top with Sulky 30 wt. Dark Tawny Tan #1057. Loosen the top tension slightly.

Joyce's Tip:
When winding any invisible thread onto a bobbin, wind slowly to avoid overstretching the thread which could break a plastic bobbin and/or result in unpleasant tension in either a metal or plastic bobbin.

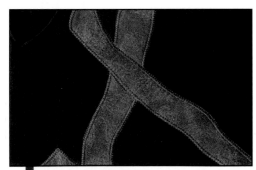

Select the Blanket Stitch if your machine has one. Other stitch choices would be an open zig-zag or blind hem (usually with invisible thread on top as well as in the bobbin).

6. Begin to Blanket Stitch

Blanket stitch around all of the branches. Then, place the one long leaf that extends above and below the animal and fuse it in place. Blanket stitch around the leaf with Sulky 30 wt. Dark Maple #1158.

Note: Using Steam-A-Seam, it is not necessary to cover the edges completely with thread because the fabric will not fray after washing, if it is properly fused down.

Peel off the nylon net from the back of the tiger, then place the tiger over the leaf and fuse it in place. Place the nylon net over the tiger and straight stitch around the outside edge with Sulky Smoke Invisible Thread on the top and in the bobbin. Thread the top with Sulky 30 wt. Black #1005, and blanket stitch around the animal. Position remaining leaves using the placement diagram, or create your own look; fuse them in place. Blanket Stitch using Sulky 30 wt. Dark Maple #1158.

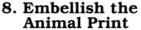

7. Create Vein Lines in the Leaves

Use a white chalk marker to draw vein lines in large leaves. Stitch vein lines using Sulky 30 wt. Dark Maple #1158 and a small satin stitch.

Joyce's Tip:
When using Sliver thread, use a Metallica 12/80 Needle or at least a 14/90 Top Stitch Needle. Also, lower your top tension dramatically. Place the spool on a __vertical__ spool pin only.

8. Embellish the Animal Print

Set up for Free-Motion:
• Drop your Feed Dogs
• Put on a Darning Foot
• Straight Stitch Setting

Embellish your Animal by using Sulky Sliver Metallic Bronze #8006 to highlight eyes and whiskers, and Sulky Sliver Metallic Opalescent #8040 to highlight the white fur areas on the tiger.

9. Serge Side Seams

Serge or sew the side seams back up and, voila, you are done!

Some bugle and seed beads were sewn onto this sweater to dress it up a little. Have fun! It's your sweater, decorate it to your taste.

Artistic Applique

A Totally Stable™ Iron-On Stabilizer Tip

Kathy Lengyel
Dunedin, FL

Machine applique pillowcases, flat sheets, towels and window valances all with the use of flat sheets and some scraps of fabric.

Trace the applique pieces from the pattern onto a fusible web, then iron into place. To keep the sheets feeling soft, adhere Sulky Totally Stable Iron-On Tear Away Stabilizer behind the area to be machine appliqued.

Kathy is a national illustrator/designer using her painterly stitched machine applique technique on the covers of romance novels, children's school books and advertising for corporations. She also has a complete pattern line called Artistic Applique which use her machine applique technique for beginners and advanced sewers.

The machine applique in this project uses different colored Sulky threads to create a painterly effect. The thread colors are changed to represent the highlights and shadows, and to add dimension to the applique border.

Set the sewing machine to zig-zag satin stitching with the stitch wide at 0 (lowest setting) and the length at satin or 1/2 (.5) and make 2-3 stitches to lock the beginning stitches. Then, increase the width to 1.5 to 2.0 (test your machine for best results). To lock the end stitches, decrease the width back to 0 and take 2-3 stitches. Clip threads.

Pattern used: Home Comfort - Artistic Applique by Kathy Lengyel Designs

The Totally Stable prevents any puckering that might happen from machine appliqueing a lot of pieces close together. When finished, simply tear away the stabilizer and the results are a nice, smooth finish that is perfect for home decorating.

Photo Transfer on Fabric *by Patsy Shields*

A Totally Stable™ Iron-on Tear-Away Stabilizer Idea

You will need:

✔ **Sulky Totally Stable**
    2 pieces cut to 8 1/2" x 11" each
✔ White Fabric cut to 8 1/2" x 11"
✔ Computer with a Flat-Bed
    or Hand-Held Scanner
✔ Ink-jet or Bubble-Jet Color Printer

(This ink may not be permanent. Do not wash!)

Instructions:

1. Press with an iron to fuse both pieces of Totally Stable to the wrong side of the fabric, one layer at a time. Also, press from the top to remove any wrinkles.
2. Following the computer manufacturer's instructions, scan your design into the computer.

3. Place the stabilized fabric in the printer.

4. Print the design onto the fabric. You may have to "guide" it when it first begins to feed.

5. When the image is printed on the fabric, embellish it with thread painting techniques, fabric markers, buttons, doilies, clothing scraps, or other memorabilia.

Great Project Ideas to Stabilize with Sulky Sticky

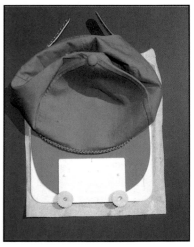

Malah Peterson
*National Sulky Educator
and Commercial
Embroiderer*

For the past 15 years, Malah has taught classes in machine applique, machine embroidery, tailoring, Ultra Suede, pants fitting and professional techniques as well as sewing machine and serger instruction. For five of those years, she was a Sewing Machine Dealer in Oregon. She confesses that her first love is teaching others and inspiring them to realize the creative potential in themselves. Her teaching is full of enthusiasm which is reflected in her goal of making sewing FUN for everyone.

"Sulky Sticky is a wonderful tool for stabilizing items that are too small or unusual to be put in a hoop when you want to do decorative stitching or embellishment on them. My husband and I have a commercial embroidery shop in our home. We use Sulky Sticky when we are embroidering or monogramming baseball caps, neckties, award ribbons, socks, shirt collars and cuffs; we have even used it to embroider a horse bridle and the ear of a large, stuffed fur animal. Home sewers can also enjoy the convenience of using Sticky. If you own one of the home-style professional embroidery machines, use Sticky when you embroider baseball caps, patches, labels, dog collars --- the list goes on and on. I especially like to use Sticky to embellish velvet, velour, polar fleece, or any fabric that may develop hoop marks when put in a hoop. With Sticky you can embroider by using only the bottom hoop thereby eliminating the top hoop that could mark the fabric. Sticky also makes it easy to embellish small or unusual items using the decorative stitches on a regular sewing machine. Use a hardwood machine embroidery hoop on which you have made marks at 'North', 'South', 'East', and 'West' to help you align things like ribbons, labels, etc. Home embroidery machine hoops already have these marks on them. You can also use Sticky with no hoop at all when you are doing something larger or longer than would normally fit into the parameters of a hoop. Simply cut a strip the length and width you need, peel off the backing, place the fabric on the sticky side, and let the feed dogs feed the fabric through normally." --- Malah

Modeled by Adam Drexler

**100
Sticky**

General Directions for using Sticky to stabilize fabric to achieve professional-looking embroidery.

When embroidering a hat, a HOOP-IT-ALL™ Hoop can make it easier.

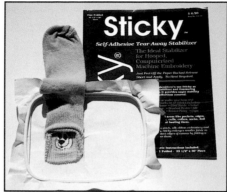

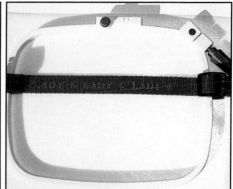

When embroidering socks, to keep the ribbing from stretching out of shape as you embroider, place the cuff against the Sticky so you will be embroidering toward the cuff edge. Pin back the rest of the sock out of the way. Remember that the cuff gets turned down when it is worn, so be mindful as to the directional placement of a single embroidered design. If stitching a decorative design all the way around the sock, you will need to tear away some of the Sticky as you progress. Continue sticking down the cuff edge as you stitch around the sock.

General Directions for using Sticky to stabilize fabric for Free-Motion Embroidery.

The little doily was done in a regular free-motion embroidery hoop stuck to Sticky so that the hoop gives you something to hold onto while working the silk ribbon roses. Since the collar on the blouse won't fit in a hoop, sticking it onto Sticky will hold it in place while doing the decorative flower or the silk ribbon embroidery. Malah prefers peeling off the release paper and sticking the hoop right onto Sticky rather than hooping the Sticky, scoring the release paper, and peeling it away.

Hoop-It-All is a trademark of the Hoop-It-All Company.

Verna Erickson

*Singer Sewing
Machine Company
Educational Consultant
from Harlan, Iowa*

Verna Erickson started
her sewing career with
the Sew/Fit company,
presenting seminars
throughout the Mid-
west. Verna's sample
garments have been
featured in conven-
tions, fashion shows
and advertising
throughout the U.S.
She has also worked
with 4-H clubs in Iowa
for a number of years.
She learned to sew as
a child, and sewing has
always been a source of
pride and enjoyment,
as well as a very inter-
esting career.

Veronica's Napkins

A Sulky Sticky™ Self-Adhesive Tear-Away Stabilizer Project

"I used Sulky Sticky for this project because Sticky makes it easy to center the area to be embroidered, even when the fabric is too small to be hooped. Sulky Sticky does not leave a residue and does not gum up the needle. It is strong enough to do baseball caps or gentle enough for chiffon." ---Verna

You will need:

✔ **Sulky Sticky Stabilizer**
✔ Sulky 40 wt.
   Rayon Threads:
   • 1049 - Grass Green
   • 1176 - Med. Dk.
     Avocado
   • 1169 - Bayberry Red
   • 1122 - Purple

✔ Sulky White Polyester
   Bobbin Thread
✔ 4 to 8 napkins
✔ Singer Quantum XL100
✔ Singer Veronica
   Card #11

All Projects were Embroidered using the Singer Quantum XL100 Embroidery Card #11 using Sulky Rayon Thread

Instructions for Napkins:

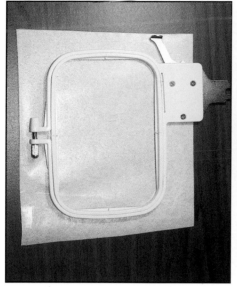

1. Preparing the hoop: Hoop Sulky Sticky Stabilizer with the release paper side up. Score the release paper with a small knife or straight pin. (Verna prefers the straight pin method.) Peel off the release paper. The Sulky Sticky becomes the stabilizer as well as holding the fabric exactly where you want it! Optional: Remove the release paper and adhere to underside of hoop as shown in picture.

2. Placing the fabric: Press the corner of the napkin onto the Sticky layer. The Singer Quantum XL 100 always centers the design, but you can move the center point by using the directional arrows until the design is in the desired area. Check positioning using the range key.

3. Sewing the design: Select the design so that it appears on the upper LCD window showing the separation of thread colors and the order in which they will be sewn. Thread the top with Sulky 40 wt. Grass Green #1049, and the bobbin with Sulky White Bobbin Thread. Touch the red start button to sew until color #1 is finished. Change the top thread to Sulky Med. Dk. Avocado #1176 and sew color #2. Continue changing the top thread as you sew the rest of the design.

Shown here and on the facing page are some additional projects created by Verna using the Veronica Card #11. The Mixer Cover and Placemat were purchased and then embroidered.

Sulky Pieced Pet Vest

by Joyce Drexler
As presented on the PBS TV Show,
SEW CREATIVE with Donna Wilder

A Sulky Sticky™ Self-Adhesive Tear-Away Stabilizer Project

"This idea began as a birthday gift project for my friend and pet groomer, Sharon Jordan, when I saw this adorable dog and cat fabric print collection designed by Debbie Mumm for M & M Fabrics. Of course, you could do the same type of patchwork featuring your favorite pet in fabric prints such as horses, fish, frogs, etc. or by making your own fabric from color photos of your pets.

To begin, choose the style of vest pattern that works best for you. On the show, I wore the Alonga Vest Pattern by Design Concepts; the sample on the right, modeled by Loretta, is from In Cahoots basic vest pattern. I showed two different vest styles on the show so viewers could see other possibilities for designing wearable art patchwork. I also took into consideration that not everyone owns a computerized sewing machine capable of stitching embroidery designs like those featured on our vests which were done with the New Home Memory Cards # 16 (Cats) and #23 (Dogs). So I wanted you to see that the Pet Vests could be made with or without the embroidery design patches."
--- Joyce

Modeled by Loretta Durian.

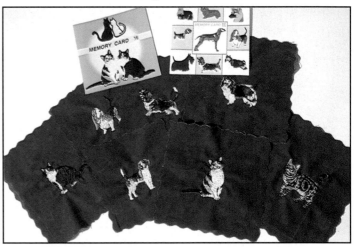

1. CREATE YOUR EMBROIDERED DESIGN

To construct your patchwork strip featuring an EMBROIDERED DESIGN:

A. First look at your fabric coordinates and choose a solid fabric as the background for your embroidered Pet Motif, one that best sets off the colors in the design.

B. Cut a piece large enough to fit in your machine's embroidery hoop.

C. Adhere Sulky Sticky Stabilizer to the bottom of the hoop.

D. Hoop the fabric and embroider your chosen design following manufacturer's directions.

2. CREATE A STRIP OF PATCHWORK.

While the embroidery is being stitched out, create some of the adjoining patchwork.

A. Cut 6-10 --- 1 1/2" x 45" strips of coordinating fabric.

B. Using your 1/4" presser foot, sew the strips together lengthwise with a 1/4" seam. PRESS SEAMS OPEN. Turn the pieced strips over and PRESS again from the right side. DO NOT IRON. Sliding the iron over these strips can cause stretching and warping of the sewn piece.

C. Using your rotary cutter, mat and ruler, trim one end even.

D. Cut several 1 1/2" strips across the stripped fabric and sew end to end until you have made a strip long enough to run the length of your vest.

E. Create 4-6 of these pieced strips - 1 1/2" x length of your vest. Set aside.

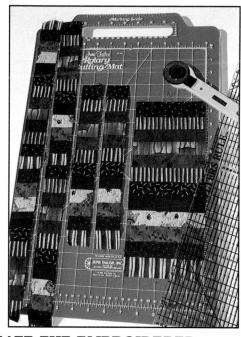

3. CREATE THE EMBROIDERED FOCAL PIECED PATCHWORK

approximately 7 1/2" wide (depending on the size of your vest and fabric print you have chosen) x the length of your vest.

A. Center the embroidered cat or dog as you trim the design piece to about 2 1/2" x 3 3/4" (or whatever size works best for the design used). Remove excess stabilizer.

B. PRESS SEAMS OPEN.

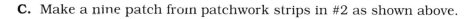

C. Make a nine patch from patchwork strips in #2 as shown above.

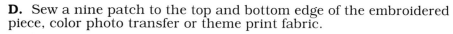

D. Sew a nine patch to the top and bottom edge of the embroidered piece, color photo transfer or theme print fabric.

E. Add a coordinating "theme print" strip across the bottom and/or top of the pieced strip.

F. PRESS SEAMS OPEN.

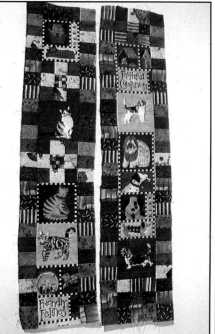

Note: If you don't have an embroidery machine, take color photos of your pets to a print shop that can make color transfers. Take white fabric for them to transfer the image onto and use the transfer instead of an embroidery.

G. Continue adding pieced coordinates or printed fabrics to this focal strip as needed for the length you desire. PRESS SEAMS OPEN.

Two ideas for pieced sections to add:
Cut 1 1/2" strips from Strip Set "A" at a 45° angle. Piece slanted strips together, off-setting colors.

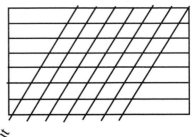

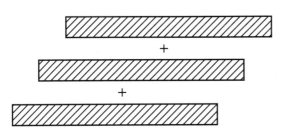

H. Add pieced strips (from 2-E) to the long sides of the finished pieced focal strip in the length needed for the vest pattern of your choice.

I. From a contrasting fabric, cut two strips of 1 1/4" x the length of the pieced focal strip. Fold wrong sides together. Match raw edge of long strip to the raw edge of the pieced focal strip. Pin. Seam together using 1/4" seam allowance.

4. SEAM PAW PRINT FABRIC TO EACH SIDE OF THE FOCAL STRIP, keeping the folded strip sandwiched. Place the vest pattern front piece over pieced front and trim to vest size.

5. ADDING POCKETS.
If using the Alonga Vest Pattern, you can add a pocket at the bottom. The pocket can also be pieced and/or embellished with machine monogrammed words relating to your pet. To monogram the pocket, back the pocket fabric with Sulky Sticky Stabilizer. Program words into the machine. Put the backed fabric in a machine hoop as desired for placement of words.

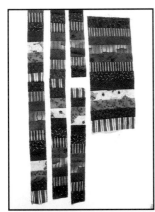

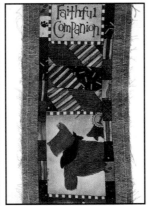

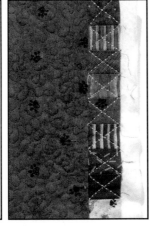

Once stitched, remove stabilizer. With right sides of lining and monogrammed pocket fabric together, seam across the top. Turn right side out. Using a scant 1/8" seam, stitch the pocket to the vest front.

6. QUILT THE VEST FRONTS.
Lay the cut front pieces over fleece and pin together with safety pins. Use Sulky Sliver or Sulky 30 wt. Rayon Thread and a 3.0 straight stitch to quilt an eighth inch from seams and across the pieced 1 1/2" strips, making X's. Stitch continuously from corner to corner going in one direction, then repeat on the way back, completing the X. You could also do free-motion serpentine quilting over the paw print fabric.

Faux Smocking by Machine

by Donna Hoeflinger

A Sulky Sticky™, Totally Stable and Solvy Stabilizer Project

You will need:

- ✔ **Sulky Sticky Stabilizer**
- ✔ **Sulky Solvy Stabilizer**
- ✔ **Sulky Totally Stable Stabilizer**
- ✔ Vest Pattern of your choice
- ✔ Vest Fabric as per pattern
- ✔ Lining Fabric as per pattern
- ✔ 1 yard Pima Cotton for inserts
- ✔ 1 to 2 yds. of fusible tricot for inserts, piping and vest fronts
- ✔ 1 1/2 yds. of piping
- ✔ Husqvarna Viking #1+ Sewing Machine
- ✔ Huskylock 1002LCD Serger
- ✔ Accessory Piping Foot for Serger
- ✔ Husqvarna Viking Embroidery Card #15, Design #33
- ✔ Amanda Jane Smocking Pleater
- ✔ Pattern Tracing Paper

- ✔ #1+ Embroidery Hoop
- ✔ Sulky 40 wt. Rayon Thread Colors:
  - #1101 - True Green
  - #1231 - Med. Rose
  - #1094 - Med. Turquoise

  Sulky 30 wt. Rayon Thread is recommended for sewing basic smocking stitches or pre-programmed decorative stitches. We used #1051 - Xmas Green #1109 - Hot Pink #1122 - Purple and #1076 - Royal Blue
- ✔ Sulky Bobbin Thread, Black

Modeled by Sasha Noe.

Donna used several traditional smocking stitches, but you could also utilize some of the decorative stitches on your sewing machine. To sew on pleated fabrics, lower the presser foot pressure several settings (setting 2 on a Husqvarna Viking #1+); use a size 90 embroidery needle and 30 wt. Sulky Rayon Thread to create your design. Green Row Color #1051 = cable stitch. Pin Row Color #1109 = 2-step wave. Purple Row Color #1122 = 5-step wave. Blue Row Color #1076 = baby wave.

Instructions:

Select vest pattern of your choice. Trace and label a right and left vest front onto pattern paper. Determine the number, size and placement of pleated inserts. Draw the insert placement on the vest fronts. Onto another sheet of pattern paper, trace and label each individual pattern section allowing for seam allowances (similar to color blocking). Cut 3 - 8" x 45" pieces of fabric for inserts. Matching the 8" selvage edges, seam 2 pieces of fabric together with a narrow or rolled hem resulting in an 8" x 90" insert. Using thread to match the insert fabric, thread 16 rows on your pleater and pleat the 8" x 90" piece of fabric. Carefully remove fabric from the pleater and knot the ends securely. Arrange pleats to required/desired fullness for pleated insert. To prevent the pleats from shifting during sewing or embroidering, iron Sulky Totally Stable onto the wrong side of the pleated insert. Repeat steps above to make an 8" x 45" pleated insert. Set up the Husqvarna Viking sewing machine for embroidery using Embroidery Card #15, Design #33. Mark design placement on each pleated insert. Follow package directions to hoop Sulky Sticky stabilizer in the Plus Hoop. Finger press the smaller insert onto the Sticky stabilizer, making sure the fabric is properly aligned.

Place a layer of Sulky Solvy on top of pleated insert. Thread the top and bobbin with Sulky 40 wt. Med. Rose #1231 and stitch position #2 of design #33. Remove pleated insert from embroidery hoop and carefully remove the Sulky Sticky, Solvy and Totally Stable from the insert. Finger press the large insert into hooped Sticky, place Solvy on top, and sew design #33 in its entirety using Sulky 40 wt. colors #1101, #1231 & #1094. Remove stabilizer, then iron fusible tricot onto the back side of each insert to permanently affix the pleats. If the pleating threads match the fabric, they do not have to be removed. Fuse tricot to remaining pieces of vest front, if desired. If necessary, trim inserts to desired size. Serge short ends of inserts to secure the pleats. For this project, a 2" x 45" strip of lame was backed with fusible tricot and wrapped over 1/8" filler cord to make the piping. To facilitate making the piping, a piping foot was used on the Huskylock 1002LCD serger. Lower presser foot pressure a notch or two on your sewing machine or serger to attach the piping to each long side of the inserts. Sew vest fronts together as per your pattern design. Finish vest according to pattern instructions.

June Mellinger

Education Manager for Brother Sewing Machine Company

June holds a degree in Marketing and Business Administration. She has many years of experience working in the home sewing field and designing Color Guard Accessories. As an Educator, she conducts training seminars for Brother Pacesetter Dealers, and consumer seminars all across the country; she is featured in several instructional videos. June recently returned from New Zealand and Australia where she launched several new products for Brother.

June is a frequent contributor to many sewing publications as well as being the creator of the popular PE-SCAN book series and THE GUIDE TO YOUR IMAGINATION. Appearing on CRAFT & COMPANY was the stepping stone to being the on-screen personality for corporate sewing education videos.

You will need:
✔ Sulky Super Solvy, Sulky Sticky and Sulky Tear-Easy Stabilizer

✔ Sulky 30 wt. Rayon Threads:
1147 - Xmas Red
1001 - Bright White
1028 - Baby Blue
1082 - Ecru
1065 - Orange Yellow
1025 - Mine Gold
1076 - Royal Blue
1055 - Tawny Tan
1059 - Dk. Tawny Brown

✔ Sulky White and Black Polyester Bobbin Thread
✔ 1 Bath Towel
✔ 1/2 Yard coordinating fabric or one pre-printed pillow top
✔ Brother Pacesetter PC-8200
✔ Memory Card SA-317 - Nintendo©
✔ Large Machine Embroidery Hoop for the PC-8200

School Rest-Time "Terry Quillow"

A Sulky Super Solvy™ Water Soluble and Sulky Sticky™ Stabilizer Project

"Today's sewers have so many fabulous things with which to embellish their creations. Sulky has developed a complete line of products that make it a snap to add a distinctive look to anything you sew or embroider! A quick walk through any store today will confirm that decorative embroidery is here to stay!" --- June

Machine Set-up:

- Set up your machine for embroidery and press EMBROIDERY EDIT.
- Touch the screen where the large letters are displayed on the right side of the screen.
- Select the large "M". Use the rotation and arrow keys to position your work.
- When you are pleased with the results, press END.
- Use the next screen to select from one of the other built-in fonts. Select the second font (satin stitch block letter). Type in the letters that will finish the name "Mario". We chose the medium size letters and then used the ROTATION icon to rotate the letters 90°. Use the arrow symbols to position the letters to your liking. Press END.
- Insert Memory Card SA-317 - Nintendo into the machine and press the Card Icon on the right side of the screen.
- Select the character that you would like to have as part of the design. Move the character to the most appropriate location with the arrow symbols.
- Press END OF EDIT to bring the complete design back to the screen. At this point you can continue to edit the design, or save it to memory.

Stabilize to Embroider your design:

1. For this project we used a piece of pre-printed fabric which helped during the selection of the towel because we wanted to fold the towel vertically in three sections to be able to fold it into the finished "QUILLOW". When using an unstamped piece of fabric, fold the towel vertically in thirds, measure the width, and add 1". Using this measurement, cut a square of fabric.

2. With the right side of the towel facing you, mark the location that coincides with where the center of the "QUILLOW" will be.

3. Stabilizers are critical when it comes to embroidering a towel. You will need to use a stabilizer on both top and bottom to add dimension to the top surface as well as keep the "nubbies" from poking through the embroidery.

4. Since terry cloth towels can be bulky and sometimes difficult to secure in an embroidery hoop, here is a tip from the professionals: cut a 9" x 12" piece of Sulky Sticky Stabilizer and secure it **in** the embroidery hoop with the shiny side of the Sticky facing up.

Back View of Hoop

Sometimes I will even fold the Sticky in quarters first so that I can use the fold lines as a reference for placement within the hoop. With a pointed object, score the protective sheet of paper around the inner part of the hoop, then tear the paper away to expose the sticky side of the stabilizer.

5. Using the machine's plastic embroidery grid guide for accurate placement, press the towel against the surface. Remove the plastic grid from the hoop.

Use Super Solvy as a Topper:

Cut a 6" x 8" piece of Super Solvy and secure it to the top surface of the towel with straight pins, or baste it on. Now you are ready to embroider.

Note: If you opt to use Sulky Tear-Easy Stabilizer instead of Sulky Sticky, sandwich the towel between the Tear-Easy and Super Solvy and secure all three layers within the embroidery hoop.

If the reverse side of the embroidery will be concealed by the "QUILLOW", use Sulky Polyester Bobbin Thread in the bobbin. If the reverse side will show, match the bobbin thread to the towel. For a reversible look, match the bobbin thread to the top threads, being sure to trim the threads each time there is a color change.

Embroider your Design:

1. Thread the top with your first color of Sulky 30 wt. Rayon thread. Attach the hoop to your PC-8200 and press START. *NOTE: When you have finished embroidering the large "M", press LAYOUT, HELP, FORWARD SEARCH until you pass over the flowers that usually embellish the Large Letters' font that is built into the PC-8200. Press RETURN, START and you will continue to embroider the lettering for "MARIO". Continue until the design is complete; change Sulky 30 wt. thread colors as you go. Lift the hoop off of the embroidery arm bracket. Carefully pull the towel away from the Sulky Sticky Stabilizer so you can patch the hole in the center of the Sticky stabilizer and use it again. Follow the directions on the Sulky Super Solvy package to remove the excess from the top of the towel.*

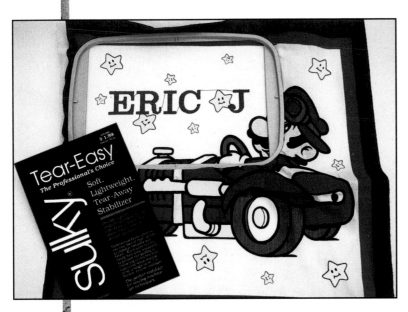

2. Embroider the child's name onto the fabric chosen for the "QUILLOW", using Sulky Tear-Easy to stabilize from the underside. Press under 1/2" on all four sides of the "QUILLOW" fabric. Hem or topstitch the top end before attaching the "QUILLOW" to the towel as you would attach a pocket to a shirt. With the embroidery facing up, fold the towel in thirds vertically. Fold the towel lengthwise to insert it into the "QUILLOW"... then off to preschool!

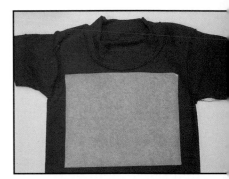

A QUICK SUPER SOLVY PROJECT:

Put a piece of Super Solvy in the PC-8200 regular embroidery hoop and attach the hoop to the machine. Take two smaller pieces of Super Solvy with a piece of tulle or netting sandwiched between them, and slide them beneath the center of the hoop. Select and embroider a character (for best results, use one of the larger designs and Sulky 30 wt. Rayon Thread). When you have finished, remove the design from the hoop. Carefully tear or trim away the excess. These make cute and quiet toys for rest time. They can also be used with a felt board to tell a story. Make a matching shirt just for fun!

Applique and Machine Embellished Denim Shirt

Featured in the book, **Applique in a Day**

A Sulky Tear-Easy™ and Solvy™ Water Soluble Stabilizer Applique & Embellishment Tip

Jackie Dodson
LaGrange
Park, IL

Previously a high school teacher, Jackie is now a full-time writer and designer who has authored or co-authored eighteen books for Chilton Book Co., as well as written numerous magazine and newsletter articles and regular columns for the American Sewing Guild in Chicago, The Needlework Times, and The Creative Machine Newsletter. She also conducts lectures and seminars for guilds, sewing machine dealers, fabric stores, and national sewing and craft organizations. Sew and Serge Terrific Textures is part of the Sew and Serge series she is writing with co-author, Jan Saunders.

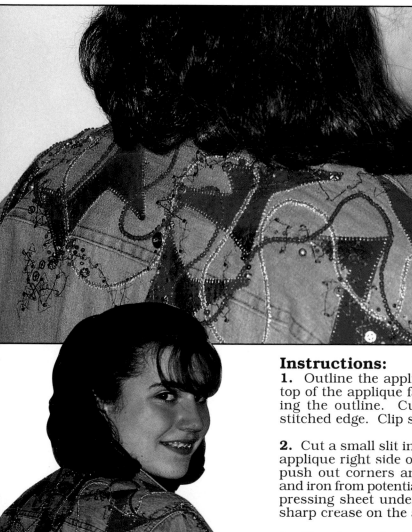

You will need:
- ✔ Sulky Tear-Easy
- ✔ Sulky Solvy
- ✔ Gold Sulky Sliver™ Metallic Thread
- ✔ Teflon Pressing Sheet
- ✔ Gluestick or Sulky KK 2000 Temporary Spray Adhesive
- ✔ Hemostat or Stuff-It Tool
- ✔ Open Toe Applique Foot

Instructions:

1. Outline the applique shape on Solvy, then pin this on top of the applique fabric. Straight stitch together, following the outline. Cut around applique 1/8" outside the stitched edge. Clip seam allowance and trim corners.

2. Cut a small slit in the center of the stabilizer to turn the applique right side out. Use a hemostat or Stuff-It Tool to push out corners and edges. Protect your ironing board and iron from potential stabilizer residue by wrapping a teflon pressing sheet under and over the applique, then press a sharp crease on the applique edges.

3. Use gluestick to hold the applique on top of the denim shirt. (Sometimes pressing the applique-backed Solvy lightly on a base fabric adheres the applique enough to stitch it in place.) Place Sulky Tear-Easy under the denim. Attach applique with a blanket stitch using the open toe applique foot and Sulky Gold Sliver Metallic Thread.

4. Use Tear-Easy when embellishing the rest of the shirt to stabilize background fabric when using decorative stitches, sewing on beads and baubles, and applying cords.

Joyce's Tip:
Sulky KK 2000 Temporary Spray Adhesive is a faster and easier alternative to pinning or gluing, and it makes fabric repositionable.

3-D Ruffled Flowers and Leaves

A Sulky Tear-Easy™ and Solvy™ Water Soluble Stabilizer Tip

Mary Mulari
Author, Designer and Educator

Mary's interest in sewing began in 4-H Club and developed through college and several years of teaching junior high school English. A lifelong Minnesota resident, Mary now travels extensively to present creative sewing seminars. She continues to enjoy teaching to other sewing enthusiasts across the country: the world's best students, in her opinion. She has become well known for her unique applique additions to garments, ranging from sweatshirts to silks, clever gift ideas, and her inspirational and entertaining seminars. Mary has written ten sewing books and contributes to the "Sewing Update Newsletter". In addition, she has developed patterns for McCalls, tests products for the sewing industry, and appears frequently as a guest on "Sewing with Nancy" and other television sewing programs.

"With the help of two kinds of Sulky stabilizers, it's easy to create unusual appliqued flowers and leaves to attach to a jacket. This example of non-traditional applique adds a touch of style to any plain jacket or other garment. I chose a tone-on-tone color presentation, selecting a variety of blue fabrics that match or nearly match the jacket. From the skirt that matches the jacket, I cut off one of the inside pockets to get enough for a matching flower and leaf. The other fabric selections are taffeta, polished cotton, and a piece of leftover ribbing cut from a ready-to-wear sweatshirt." --- Mary

You will need:

✔ **Sulky Tear-Easy Stabilizer and Sulky Solvy Stabilizer**
✔ Sulky Rayon Threads:
   • 30 weight to coordinate with your fabric choice
   • 40 weight to match 30 weight color(s)
✔ Sulky Iron-On Transfer Pen
✔ Zig-zag Sewing Machine
✔ Machine Needle 14/90
✔ 1 Yard 3/8" Wide Clear Elastic
✔ Buttons for the Center of each Flower
✔ Straight Pins or Applique Pins
✔ 1/4 Yard Lightweight Tricot Fusible Interfacing
✔ 4 1/2" Squares of Fabric for Flowers & Leaves

Mary Mulari shows you how to give a new look to a ready-made jacket with 3-D applique. Modeled by Patti Lee.

Instructions:

1. With a Sulky Iron-On Transfer Pen, trace the patterns for the flower and leaf from the pullout pattern sheet onto plain paper.

2. Fuse lightweight tricot interfacing to the wrong sides of the squares of applique fabric.

3. On the jacket featured, there are five flowers and three leaves. Decide how many of each you will make for your project, then, using a dry iron at a temperature suitable for the fabric, transfer the two designs that many times onto the interfaced sides of the fabrics, and cut out the shapes.

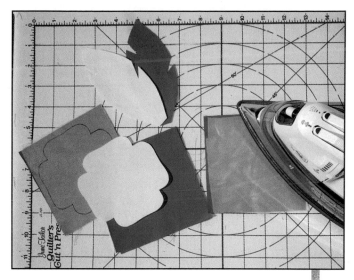

4. Cut pieces of both Solvy and Tear-Easy Stabilizers slightly larger than the flower and leaf shapes. This combination of stabilizers produces a firm stitching base which, after sewing, can be easily removed, leaving a clean edge on the appliques.

5. Pin the flowers and leaves right side up on top of the Solvy and Tear-Easy pieces. Keep the pin heads in the center of the shapes to avoid obstructions while sewing, or use shorter applique pins to hold the fabric to the stabilizers.

6. Thread the machine with Sulky 30 wt. Rayon Thread, and fill a bobbin in a 40 wt. thread color to match the Sulky top thread. Select an applique stitch. For the leaves on the jacket, Mary used a standard satin stitch, but she chose an alternate stitch for the flowers. Check your machine to see the choices for a variety stitch around the edges of the designs.

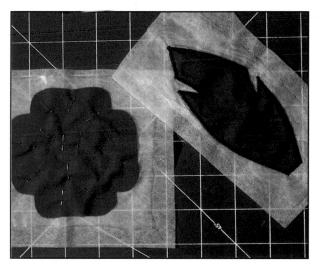

7. Before stitching around the flowers and leaves, you may want to practice the stitching on fabric and stabilizer scraps, and alter the stitch width and length. Then sew around the edges of each flower and leaf. Draw the threads to the underside of the shapes.

8. Now, remove the stabilizers carefully so you won't distort the applique stitches or the shapes. First tear or cut away the layers *inside* the flower and leaf shapes. Then remove the Tear-Easy layer from around the edges of the designs. Remove the Solvy layer from around the edges last. You may wish to wet the edges to remove the last bits of Solvy.

9. To gather the flowers and leaves, cut 2" long pieces of clear elastic, two pieces for each flower and one piece for each leaf. Thread top and bobbin with the Sulky 40 wt. (from #6 above) and turn each flower over to sew on the wrong side with a narrow zig-zag stitch on the lines shown on the pattern pieces to secure the elastic strips, stretching the elastic as you sew. Sew a second piece of elastic on the second line shown on the pattern, across the first row of elastic. Suddenly, you have flower shapes that are more interesting than the simple flat shapes!

10. To gather the leaves, begin sewing the elastic at the short, straight end of the leaf and stretch and sew the elastic down to about 2/3 the length of each leaf.

11. The design shapes are all set to be stitched to the garment you've chosen to decorate. The best way to plan their arrangement is to try on the garment and pin on the shapes while you are looking in the mirror. Use the featured jacket arrangement as an inspiration for your design layout.

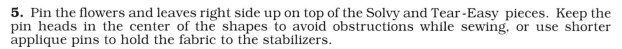

12. On the underside of the garment, beneath the area of the design arrangement, pin a large piece of Tear-Easy Stabilizer to prepare for sewing the designs in place.

13. Use the Sulky 40 wt. thread and a narrow zig-zag stitch to sew the shapes to the jacket. Stitch over the zig-zag seams that attached the elastic to the wrong side of the flowers and leaves. Remove the pins and then the stabilizer on the wrong side of the garment.

14. For an additional accent, sew buttons to the center of each flower. Mary covered buttons, using the taffeta fabric for all five buttons.

15. Don't forget to add your signature tag to the garment. Mary used a rubber stamp with her name and fabric paint to sign her name to her jacket. The same decorative stitch used for the flower edges was also used to trim the tag.

16. Now it's time to wear and enjoy the dimensional applique display you've created on your jacket. Consider this design project for other clothing too, or a coordinating hat.

Totally Stable
"Sheer Magic Jacket"

By the Author of "Thread Magic-
The Enchanted World of Ellen Anne Eddy"
Photos by Ellen Eddy

"I use Sulky Totally Stable to draw out all of my animals and creatures in my quilts. I love to embroider them separately on hand-dyed cotton from the back with the Totally Stable ironed on as my pattern. The hummingbird and flowers were all drawn and embroidered on Totally Stable. I also used Sulky Solvy as the stabilizer for the 3-D Butterflies in my book. In the hoop, I used 2 layers of tulle, 2 layers of Solvy, or 1 layer of Super Solvy, and my drawing on Totally Stable. I embroidered the butterflies, cut them out and bound them with a machine buttonhole stitch." --- Ellen

Ellen Anne Eddy
*Author, Fiber Artist
from Chicago, IL*

Ellen has spent most of her life either teaching, writing or working with fabric, and now she's come to a point where all occupations blend. She began quilting in response to a gift from a neighbor who saved a quilt top from one of her mother's cleaning fits, and gave it to Ellen to quilt when she was grown. It was such an inspiration that she has been quilting ever since. She currently teaches a series of fiber art courses called "Thread Magic", covering all kinds of machine embroidery techniques for quilters. She lives in Chicago with four cats who are all very involved with Ellen's work, and have long since taken over quality control.

For the Sheer Jacket to the left you will need:

✔ **A Zig-Zag Sewing Machine**
  • Machine Needle
    Size 80/12 or 90/14
  • Edge Foot, Darning Foot
✔ **Sulky Stabilizers:**
  Super Solvy™ and
  Totally Stable™
✔ **A Jacket Pattern -**
    with Dolman Sleeves
✔ **Fabric:** Various Green Organzas
  • Purple Organza for Jacket body in fabric amounts as pattern suggests
✔ **Hummingbird/Leaf Design -**
    on Pullout Pattern Sheet
✔ **Notions:**
  • Teflon and Cloth
    Pressing Sheets
  • Iron & Pressing Surface
  • 8" or 10" German Hardwood
    Machine Embroidery Hoop
  • Fine-line, Permanent-Ink Marker
  • Applique Scissors, Embroidery Scissors
  • Gimp

✔ **Sulky Sliver™ Metallic**
  • 8040 - Opalescent
  • 8051 - Black
  • 8024 - Multi-Color
✔ **Sulky Threads:**
  40 wt. Sulky Rayon
  • 1005 - Black
  • 1011 - Steel Gray
  • 1236 - Lt. Silver
  • 1207 - Sea Foam Green
  • 1001 - Bright White
  • 1192 - Fuchsia
  • 1191 - Dk. Rose
  • 1517 - Coachman Green
  • 1096 - Dk. Turquoise
  • 1513 - Turquoise
  • 1046 - Teal
  • 1104 - Pastel Yellow/Green

1. Choose Pattern and Fabric

Choose a suitable jacket pattern and fabric. Ellen chose an out-of-print Simplicity Pattern for her jacket for several reasons: there are only 4 pattern pieces which gave her larger flat areas for embroidering; there are no gathered seams or darts; since Ellen is short-waisted, a short dolman jacket was most flattering. Her fabric of choice was a light, shiny purple organza, since organza has more internal stability than other sheers such as voile or chiffon.

2. Cut Out Pattern and Sew Seams

Cut out the pattern twice in the organza. One is for the outside of your jacket and the other is for the lining. Sew the shoulder seams and the back seams (if any) of each layer. Finish them by using an edging stitch and trimming away any extra. Lay these pieces aside while you prepare the hummingbird embroidery.

3. Trace the Hummingbird onto Totally Stable Iron-on Stabilizer

With a fine-point pencil or pen, trace the Hummingbird (see pullout pattern) onto Totally Stable. Use this firm tear-away stabilizer for several reasons. It irons on, which is important because it protects the design from shifting while stitching on such an ephemeral fabric as organza. It has an excellent surface on which to draw; the top side of Totally Stable is like a fine-weight, non-woven interfacing, and takes pencil drawing extremely well, but it has the added feature of being able to tear away when the embroidery is completed.

4. Prepare to Stitch the Hummingbird

Since the Hummingbird is to be solidly filled in, it will need additional stabilization. On an ironing surface, first place 2 layers of organza, then 2 layers of Super Solvy, followed by the Totally Stable (fusible side down) with pattern traced on it. With your iron set on a temperature suitable for organza, move it swiftly over the Totally Stable to fuse it to the top layer of Super Solvy; place this stack in a machine embroidery hoop for free-motion embroidery --- therefore working the Hummingbird upside down. *Your embroidery will be in reverse on the face of the jacket organza. Ellen feels that working from the back allows her to constantly see her design and she can knot off her thread ends to stabilize them as well. Although, as the piece develops, she will also work from the front.*

5. Set up your machine for Free-Motion Embroidery

A. Lower or cover the feed dogs.
B. Attach a free-motion darning foot.
C. Insert a size 14/90 embroidery needle.
D. Thread the top with Sulky 40 wt. #1005 Black, and the bobbin with Black Sulky Bobbin Thread. Select a small width zig-zag stitch. Loosen top tension slightly.

6. Embroider the Hummingbird -

Beginners to Free-Motion Embroidery should refer to the "Embroidery Concepts in Sulky" Book.

A. Begin to embroider by stitching an outline in a sliding side-stitch motion. *Note: Thread colors that follow will be placed in both the bobbin and needle.*
B. The rest of the bird will also be stitched in 40 wt. Sulky Rayon. Shade the wings, tail, tummy and beak with Steel Gray #1011.
C. Continue shading the wings and tummy with Lt. Silver #1236.
D. Add a green tone using Sea Foam Green #1207.

E. Finish filling in the body with White #1001.
F. Use Fuchsia #1192 to under-shade the head, and Dk. Rose #1191 to fill in the head.
G. Shade the body with Coachman Green #1517, then add Dk. Turquoise #1096.
H. Finish filling in with Turquoise #1513.

I. Stitch the eye of the Hummingbird in Sulky *Sliver* because the sheen of this flat, brilliant thread creates an illusion of a wet surface, like an eye. Use Black #8051 for the pupil and Opalescent #8040 for the gleam in the eye. Remove from hoop and set aside.

7. Prepare to Embroider the Outside of the Jacket

A. Using a fine-line, permanent-ink marker, trace the vines and leaves from the pull-out pattern onto Totally Stable, and iron it (watch your iron temperature) onto the underside of the jacket pieces so they won't shift while embroidering. You will completely remove the excess Totally Stable after embroidering, leaving the jacket sheer and lovely.
B. Cut strips of Totally Stable and iron them over the underarm seams so, as you bring the embroidery across the shoulder line (one of the main visual areas on a sheer jacket), your embroidery will stitch out perfectly!
C. Secure the inside of your jacket in a machine embroidery hoop to stitch all of the stems and leaves. (Again, you will be working from the wrong side (underside) so put the same color thread in both top and bobbin.)

8. Embroider the Outside of the Jacket

A. Using Coachman Green #1517, stitch the vines and leaves with a slanted sideways zig-zag stitch. Use a straight stitch to make the veins in the leaves.
B. Using the same stitches, add more leaves and vines in Teal Green #1046.
C. Finish the plain vines and leaves with a Pastel Yellow Green #1104.
D. Add small blossoms with Fuchsia #1192.

9. Attach the Hummingbird to the Jacket Back

A. Pin the Hummingbird in place on the outside of the jacket back and secure it in an embroidery hoop. With Sulky #1005 Black, outline the Hummingbird with a free-motion straight stitch. Cut away the extra organza from the Hummingbird motif, *leaving about a half inch border around it.* Tear away the excess Totally Stable and cut away all of the left-over Solvy.

B. Trim away the remaining 1/2" of organza from the edges of the Hummingbird up to the straight stitch outline.

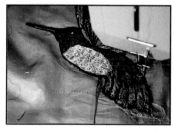

C. Using a free-motion slanted zig-zag stitch, encase the edges of the Hummingbird.

10. Applique Leaves

A. Choose a selection of green organzas for the appliqued leaves. Because the organza is sheer, you can see through it to see the leaf patterns drawn on the Totally Stable. On the outside of the jacket, place a square of organza (slightly larger than the leaf) each place where you want a leaf to be. Free-motion straight stitch around each leaf with Sulky #1517 Coachman Green.

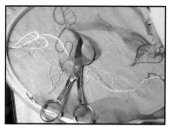

B. Trim away the organza from the leaf shape, up to the stitching line.

C. Stitch over the straight stitching with a small slanted zig-zag, sliding (not pivoting) around the leaf shape.

D. Add finishing details to the veins with a free-motion straight stitch.

11. Stipple Quilt the Jacket

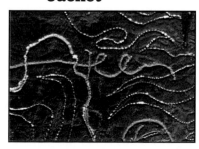

A. Once all the leaves are finished, put Multi-color Sliver #8024 in the bobbin and White Rayon #1001 in the needle (Ellen often works with Sliver in the bobbin because she experiences less breakage that way). Since you are using a straight stitch, you don't necessarily need to use a hoop to stipple quilt around all of the leaves from the underside.

12. Finish the Jacket Construction

A. Tear away the rest of the stabilizer from the jacket. Sew and finish the underarm seam on both the lining and outside of the jacket. Pin the lining to the edges of the jacket sleeves and the edges running around the front to the back so that there are no raw seams showing except at the edges.

B. To create an edge, stabilize the edge with Totally Stable. Then, using Coachman Green #1517 and a buttonhole stitch, zig-zag the edge over gimp.

C. Tear or cut away the excess stabilizer along the edge.

D. Buttonhole stitch or blanket stitch the edge of the jacket.

"Morning Glories" from Ellen's Book ---"THREAD MAGIC" - The Enchanted World of Ellen Eddy, Published by "Fiber Studio Press".

To make this Child's Beanie Baby™ Carrier you will need:

✔ **Sulky 40 wt. Rayon:**
   Select colors according to
   embroidery designs chosen

✔ **Sulky Stabilizers:**
   • 1 package **Totally Stable** ™
   • 2 packages **Tear-Easy**™

✔ **A New Home Memory Craft 9000
   Sewing Machine and Embroidery Hoop**
   • Memory Card #112 (Farm Animals)
   • Memory Card #23 (Dog Series)
   • Memory Card #30 (Wildlife Series)
   • Machine Blue Tip Needle Size 11/75
   • Edge Foot, Darning Foot, "A" Foot

✔ **Notions:**
   • Fabric Marker
   • 3 yds. - 1/4" or 3/8" elastic
   • 2 1/2 yds. - 1" Ribbon
   • Washable Fabric Marker
   • 1/2 yd. - Fusible Interfacing
   • Regular Sewing Thread to match
     chosen fabrics

✔ **Fabric:**
   • 1 yd. Novelty Print (Outside of Bag)
   • 2 yds. Lt. Wt. Denim or Contrasting
     Cotton for the inside of bag and
     handles
   • 1 yd. contrasting cotton (pockets)

✔ **Fabric Cutting:**
   • From Novelty Print:
     2 - 12 1/2" x 20 1/2" strips
     for outside of front and back
   • From Denim:
     2 - 15" x 20 1/2" strips
      for inside of front and back
     2 - 8 1/2" x 15" strips (Ends)
     2 - 8 1/2" x 20 1/2" strips
     (bottom - inside and outside)
     2 - 4" x 20 1/2" strips
     (handles)
   • From contrasting Cotton (Pockets):
     8 - 9" x 27 1/2" strips
     (outside pockets and lining)
     4 - 9" x 12 1/2" strips
     (end pockets and lining)

"Beanie Baby™ Carrier"

A Totally Stable™ and Tear Easy™ Embroidery Project

Every child has stuffed toys laying every-where. Pockets all the way around and on the inside gives a home for 16 of your child's Beanie Babies.

Prepare the Pockets for Professional-Style Embroidery on the Memory Craft 9000.

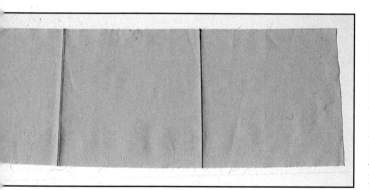

1. Fold four of the eight pocket strips into thirds and press the folds. (Two for the outside bag and two for the inside. The remaining four strips will be used to line the pockets.) On right side of fabric, mark pressed lines with a washout fabric marker to divide the pockets into one-third sections. (Later, these lines will become stitching lines.) In the center of each of these sections is the perfect palette for embroidery. In the samples sewn, New Home Memory Cards #112 (Farm Designs), #30 (Wildlife Series) and #23 (Dog Series) were used.

Several of the pocket sections feature designs that were combined on the Memory Craft's Edit Screen without "rehooping" the fabric. Try combining the barn, fence and pig from Memory Card #112.

2.
- Iron a 6" x 8" piece of fusible interfacing to the center of the wrong side of each of the pocket sections.
- Iron a 4" x 6" piece of **Totally Stable** over the center of the interfacing.
- Place one of the pocket sections in the embroidery hoop, and place the hoop on the carriage.
- Select desired design. Before beginning to sew, slide 2 layers of **Tear-Easy** under the hoop.

If you are combining designs by "rehooping", remove the Tear-Easy after each embroidery, then replace the Tear-Easy before sewing the next designs.

Sue Thorton-Gray
Educational Coordinator
New Home Sewing
Machine Co.

Sue has been with New Home since 1989 during which time she has conducted consumer seminars, dealer product knowledge training and represented New Home at various consumer shows. She is also responsible for planning and conducting classes at New Home Institute.

Sue has appeared on Aleene's "Creative Living with Crafts", "Crafting for the 90's", "Strip Quilting with Kaye Wood", and "Sew Creative" T.V. programs. She has also been published in several sewing related publications. Sue lives in Wisconsin with her husband, Brian, and spends her spare time enjoying her four grand-daughters. She hopes one day sewing will be as much fun to them as it is for her. Sue says, "I can't ever remember not sewing."

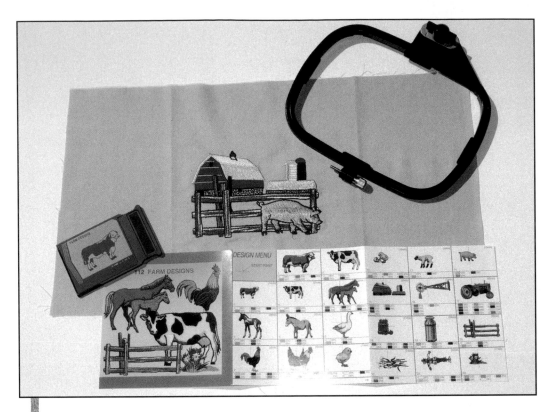

You can combine the barn, fence and pig as follows:

• Select Barn #15, press Edit Key. Press arrows to move all the way up and to the left. Sew.
• Select Fence #20, press Edit Key. Press arrows to move all the way down and to the left. Sew.
• Select Pig #14, press Edit Key. Press arrows to move all the way down and to the right. Sew.

Construction of the Bag

Note: use 1/2" seam allowance throughout.

1. Place embellished pocket and pocket lining, right sides together. Sew across the long edge using a straight stitch. Press. Repeat for all pockets, making two embellished pockets for the outside bag, **front** and **back;** two pockets, not embellished, for the inside of the bag, **front** and **back;** two embellished **end** pockets for the outside of the bag and two **end** pockets, not embellished, for the inside of the bag.

2. Cut elastic: 20" each for front and back pockets, and 9" for the end pockets. Fold and mark the 20" pieces of elastic into thirds; sew them to the seam allowance of the pockets using a multiple zig-zag stitch with the width set so that the zig-zag stitches almost to the outside edge of the elastic on both sides. Stretch as you sew, matching the marks on the elastic with the lines on the fabric. Sew the 9" pieces without folding. Flip the fabric to other side.

• Stitch the design with the appropriate Sulky 40 wt. colors.
• When sewing is completed, remove all stabilizers.
• Embellish all pocket sections, including the ends.

3. Set the Memory Craft for gathering:
• Straight Stitch #1
• Stitch Length 5.0
• Thread Tension 9
• "A" Foot

Matching the raw edges, gather the bottoms of each pocket sections.

4. Fold the two 12 1/2" x 20 1/2" novelty print strips into thirds (outside base fabric). Press a crease and mark the crease with a washout fabric marker. Repeat for the two 15" x 20 1/2" denim strips (inside base fabric).

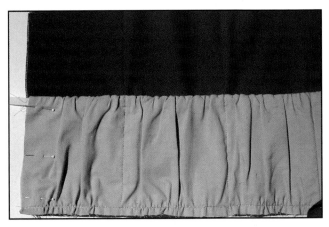

5. Pin a pocket section to an outside base piece, matching marks on the pocket with marks on the base fabric. Repeat, pinning all pocket sections to the base sections and ends.

6. Machine baste across bottom and both sides of all pieces.

7. To secure pockets to base fabric, straight stitch pocket sections on marks drawn.

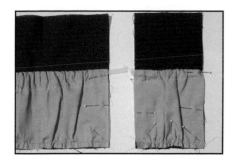

8. With the right sides together, sew both end pieces to the front and back pieces. Repeat for the inside of the bag.

Sew the bottoms to the bags

1. Start with a short side (8 1/2") of the bottom fabric piece and, with right sides together, pin it to one end of the bag. Sew from seam to seam. Next, with right sides together, sew one long side, seam to seam.

2. Sew other short end, right sides together, seam to seam. Repeat for last long side. Repeat for other bag.

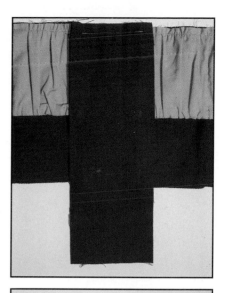

Sew the outside and inside bag together

1. Both the outside and inside bags are now completed and ready to be sewn together. Insert the inside bag into the outside bag, wrong sides together. The inside bag will extend 1 1/2" beyond the outside bag (the "extension").

Sew the handles

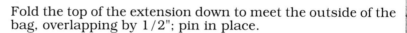

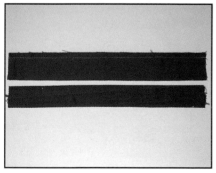

2. With wrong sides together, press under the top of the inside bag 1/2".

3. Determine the front of your bag. Find the center of the extension (see #1 to the left). With a washable fabric marker, mark placement for a 1" buttonhole. Sew the buttonhole and cut it open.

Fold the top of the extension down to meet the outside of the bag, overlapping by 1/2"; pin in place.

1. Sew the handle strip together along the long edge, right sides together. Turn. Press seam down center. Repeat for the second handle.

2. The placement of the handles are approximately 3" from each side of the center front and back. Tuck the raw edge of the handle under the extension. Topstitch in place at the top and bottom of the handle.

3. Topstitch all the way around the bottom of the bag extension to secure it to the outside of the bag. To finish off the bag, insert the ribbon in the casing created by the extension. ***Buy some Beanie Babies and place them in the pockets.***

This straw hat was created as a lark to take the stress out of yard work. Why not attract Butterflies and Hummingbirds to enjoy the *time away from the sewing machine?*

Any motif which has a dense fill-in stitch with no background fabric showing can be used. The Butterfly was created on the Pfaff Creative™ 7570, Selection #5 from the Animals Collection I. The butterfly is enlarged.

For machines which do not have an embroidery unit, similar Butterflies and Flowers can be stitched free motion. Construction will be the same technique.

Notes from Jeanie: While creating "Thread-Art" designs, I enjoy using Sulky products. There are <u>no surprises</u>, because they never fail to perform to my expectations. Sulky 30 Weight Rayons are available in such a variety of colors. This makes it easy to match my hand-dyed silk ribbons when combining machine decorative stitches with my machine embroidered silk ribbons.

I am insisting that my students use the Sulky Invisible Polyester Thread while embroidering silk ribbons by machine because it is soft enough to gently gather the ribbons without cutting into them. Lightweight Sulky Polyester Bobbin Thread is strong enough to secure the Sulky Invisible Polyester Thread, yet has no build-up on the reverse side.

To make this adorable Butterfly Attractor Hat you will need:

HAT BAND:
✔ A Straw Hat
✔ **Sulky Super Solvy Stabilizer** 10" wide and 8" longer than ribbon
✔ **Sulky Threads:** White Bobbin Thread Polyester Clear Invisible
✔ 2/3 yard 2 1/2" Wide Grosgrain Ribbon
✔ Bright 7 mm Silk Ribbons
✔ Sewing thread the color of Grosgrain Ribbon
✔ Zig-Zag Sewing Machine
✔ Machine Needle Size 70/10 for Silk Ribbon Embroidery
✔ 8 or 10" German Hardwood Machine Embroidery Hoop

BUTTERFLY:
✔ **Sulky Cut-Away Soft 'n Sheer Permanent Stabilizer -** Enough to hoop 4 times
✔ **Sulky Super Solvy Stabilizer -** 3 pieces about 2" larger than Butterfly
✔ **Sulky Threads:** 30 wt. Rayon to match Silk Ribbons White Bobbin Thread
✔ Sewing Thread - to match outline color of Butterfly
✔ Sewing Machine Needle Size 90/14
✔ Low Loft Batting - size of Butterfly
✔ 8" of Heavy Braid
✔ Oval Shaped Jewel & Pin-Back
✔ Water Soluble Pen
✔ Bent Serger Tweezers

Butterfly Attractor Hat

A Sulky Cut-Away Soft 'n Sheer™ and Super Solvy™ Stabilizer Project

"Sulky permanent Cut-Away Soft 'n Sheer is a wonderful foundation for free-motion embroidery and computerized stitching because it is strong enough to hold the built-up threads, yet pliable enough to be an excellent base. It can be used alone so there will be a more delicate, finished motif.

*Super Solvy is wonderful for making a small piece of ribbon, lace, or doily large enough to be placed in the machine embroidery hoop for embellishment. It is **super strong** and can be stretched taut in the hoop without tearing." --- Jeanie*

Jeanie Sexton
from Kuttawa, Kentucky
"Thread Art by Jeanie"

Jeanie's garments and quilts have been shown in over 35 juried fashion and fiber-art shows and exhibits. She has designed ensembles for American Quilter's Society and Fairfield Fashion Shows. Jeanie won first place in the 1995 Sulky Vest Challenge, and second place in the Wearable Category of the 1996 Sulky Challenge.

In 1996, she won first place from nearly 6,000 entries in the Wonderful Wearables Category of the Aleene's Crafter of the Year contest. Jeanie has published eleven "Unique Technique" machine art instructional patterns and a book, Silk Ribbons by Machine, published by the American Quilter's Society. She also hosts three-day retreats in her Thread Art by Jeanie studio in the woods near the lake in Kuttawa.

Instructions for Hat Band

1. To determine the size of grosgrain ribbon to cut, measure the hat crown and add about 4 extra inches. Mark motif for Silk Ribbon Embroidery on grosgrain ribbon, beginning in center and ending about an inch from end of hat measurement.

2. Center ribbon on a strip of Super Solvy that is large enough to fit into your hoop; baste edges (Sulky KK 2000 works great with no pinning). Hoop Super Solvy so that it is taut by gently pulling the edges with the ends of the ribbon while gently smoothing the wrinkles out of the Super Solvy. Stitch the vines and leaves first so you can place the hoop on a vine when repositioning it.

3. Stitch the silk ribbons onto grosgrain ribbon using instructions for simple daisies in **"Silk Ribbons by Machine"** by Jeanie Sexton; or use machine instructions by Gina Butler in the two Sulky Books --- **Patchwork Concepts 900B-9 and Embroidery Concepts 900B-10**; or stitch them by hand.

4. After embroidery is completed, pull out basting stitches (not necessary if you used KK 2000) and trim Super Solvy close to the stitches. Sponge off remaining Super Solvy and the water soluble markings from the reverse side. Fluff up petals with tip of tweezers. Allow to dry. Press grosgrain ribbon from the top side, being careful not to iron on the embroidery. Any Super Solvy remaining in the ribbons will stiffen them slightly. This is neat for crafts, however, if you want the ribbons to be soft, completely soak them in water. Using matching sewing thread, topstitch the edges of the ribbon band to the hat with a 3.0 mm straight stitch, turning in the ends at center back and butting them up against each other. Zig-zag the ends together using a 2.0 mm stitch width.

Stitch the Butterfly

1. Hoop a piece of Sulky Cut-Away Soft 'n Sheer. Set up machine so that stitch colors of your butterfly can be repeated if the stitches are not dense enough. To stitch the butterfly use the appropriate colors of Sulky 30 wt. Thread on top with Sulky Bobbin Thread in the bobbin. If there is no dense stitching to outline the butterfly, leave in hoop, return machine to normal straight stitch sewing mode and outline a couple of times with a 2.0 mm stitch length. Remove from hoop and press from wrong side on a terry towel.

2. Place butterfly, **right side down,** on another piece of Sulky Cut-Away Soft 'n Sheer and pin baste. Using sewing thread to match outline color of butterfly and a 1.5 mm stitch length, straight stitch very close around edge and across the base of the antennae which will not be used on this 3-D project. Repeat stitching a couple of times. Turn project over and repeat on top of stitches with a 1.0 mm stitch length. Trim away the Soft 'n Sheer leaving 1/4" allowance. Clip curves. Cut a slit in the middle for turning.

3. Turn right side out, being careful not to punch a hole in the Soft 'n Sheer. Pin, or use KK 2000 to spray-glue edges under so the stabilizer does not show. Lay right side up on a piece of Super Solvy that is slightly larger than the butterfly. Use the outline color of Sulky 30 wt. Thread in the needle and bobbin to satin stitch around the edge with a 2.0 mm width and 0.5 mm length, stitching off the edge onto the Super Solvy. Gently pull away the Super Solvy without pulling out stitches, or sponge the edges only.

Make a second, identical Butterfly

1. Cut a piece of batting the shape of butterfly, but about 1/2" smaller. Place butterflies **wrong sides together,** with batting inside. Pin baste. Slip an inch of the center of heavy antennae braid inside between butterflies. Underneath the butterflies, place two layers of Super Solvy about 2" larger than butterfly. To encase previous stitching, put the outline color of Sulky 30 wt. Thread in the needle and the bobbin, and use a 2.5 mm width zig-zag to satin stitch around the edges, stitching off the edge onto the Super Solvy. Gently tear away the Super Solvy. Dampen the edge to remove any whiskers.

2. Stitch a jewel in center of top butterfly and a pin-back to backside. Stiffen antennae to form curved shape by wrapping them in Super Solvy, dampening them, and allowing them to dry. Cut ends to size. *(This can be done before or after stitching them.)*

Team Spirit Album Cover

A Sulky Tear-Easy™ Lightweight Stabilizer and Sulky Puffy Foam™ Project

"I chose Sulky Tear-Easy because it is easy to use and it doesn't add bulk when you are double stitching. Sulky has many excellent stabilizers, so finding the perfect stabilizer is easy." --- Marlis

You will need:

- ✔ **Sulky Tear-Easy Stabilizer**
- ✔ **Sulky Puffy Foam** in colors to match your thread choices
- ✔ Sulky Bobbin Thread
- ✔ Photo album or binder
- ✔ 1/2 yd. of 60" woven fabric (for the sample we used a stable lightweight denim)
- ✔ 1/2 yd. of batting
- ✔ Sulky 40 wt. Rayon Thread in colors matching the school logo and mascot
- ✔ 2 yds. of piping
- ✔ Bernette Deco 600 Embroidery Machine
- ✔ Bernette Deco Scan II with blank memory card
- ✔ Bernina Serger with Multi-purpose Foot
- ✔ Bernina Sewing Machine with Bulky Overlock Foot #12 or #12C
- ✔ Standard and Large Embroidery Hoops
- ✔ Design Card #1
- ✔ Bernina Design Card #101 (Suzy's Zoo)
- ✔ Fabric Glue
- ✔ Tweezers
- ✔ Washable Fabric Marker

Marlis Bennett
of Lubbock, TX

Marlis has two passions in her life, sewing and teaching. As a Training Consultant for Bernina of America, she is able to combine the two. Before coming on board with Bernina, she taught French and German at the high school level. She has also inspired many sewing students in Lubbock, Texas, and Albuquerque, New Mexico.

A Texan by choice, she was born and raised in Europe. She and her husband have two sons.

This unique notebook cover is a great way to show school spirit. Use design cards and/or scanned designs to represent mascots and symbols. Stitch over Sulky Puffy Foam to give a permanent, bold, raised look to the design.

Spine:

1. Lay the binder flat on the right side of the fabric and draw all around the edges with a washable marker. Draw two vertical lines to mark the spine of the binder.

2. Place Tear-Easy behind the area of the fabric marking the spine and hoop them together in the large hoop with the spine area in the center.

3. Thread the top with a Sulky 40 wt. Rayon in a school color, and the bobbin with Sulky Bobbin Thread. Use an Embroidery needle size 14/90.

4. Insert Card #1 into the Deco Embroidery Machine. Program the name of the school using the script alphabet in the medium size.

5. Use the TRIAL function of the Deco 600 to check the placement of the lettering on the spine. When it is as desired, stitch the school name along the spine.

6. Release the fabric from hoop and remove as much stabilizer as possible from the back of the design.

Front:

Plan the design for the front of the cover, marking the center position of each desired design to aid you in positioning and stitching them onto the cover. On the cover shown in the photograph, the school initials, mascot name, and student initials were programmed into the Bernette Deco 600 using Design Card #1; the tiger paws were scanned using the Bernette Deco Scan II; and the tiger design representing the school mascot was taken from the Studio Bernina Design Card #101 (Suzy's Zoo).

Puffy Foam School Initials:

Using Card #1, program the initials of the school in large block letters. Adjust the thread density to the maximum setting.
• Using the standard frame, hoop the cover fabric with Tear-Easy Stabilizer behind it.
• Spray Sulky KK 2000 Temporary Spray Adhesive on the back of a piece of Puffy Foam that is slightly larger than the initials and place it on top of the fabric within the hoop.
• Embroider the initials, stitching through the Puffy Foam.
• Remove the hoop from the machine, but *do not remove the fabric from the hoop.*
• Snip the foam in all places where there were no stitches to perforate it.
• Carefully tear away the rest of the foam *without* distorting the fabric.
• Reattach the hoop to the Deco Machine.
• Stitch the design a second time over the original stitching.
• Release the fabric from the hoop and remove as much stabilizer as possible from the back of the design.
• From the wrong side of the fabric, use tweezers to pull the threads at the places where the foam was snipped. This will snug the stitches on the right side of the fabric. Secure the loose threads to the fabric on the wrong side with a dab of fabric glue.

Mascot Name:

Using card #1, program the name of the school mascot in medium size script letters.
• Using the standard frame, hoop the fabric with Tear-Easy Stabilizer under it.
• Stitch the mascot name on the front of the cover as desired.
• Release the fabric from the hoop and remove as much stabilizer as possible from the back of the design.

Student Monogram:

Using card #1, program the student's initials in the desired size of script letters.

• Using the standard frame, hoop the cover fabric with Tear-Easy Stabilizer under it.
• Stitch the initials of the student in the lower right corner of the cover.
• Release the fabric from the hoop and remove as much stabilizer as possible from the back of the design.

Mascot Design:

Select a design that represents the school to stitch on the cover.

• Using the standard frame, hoop the cover fabric with Tear-Easy Stabilizer under it. Place Puffy Foam on top of the fabric within the hoop.

• Stitch the interior portions of the design through the foam. Use the Forward Stitch function to stitch over the same areas a second time.
• Stitch the outer portions of the design (not the outline) once.
• Remove the hoop from the machine, but *do not remove the fabric from the hoop.*
• Snip the foam in all places where there were no stitches to perforate it. Carefully tear away the rest of the foam without distorting the fabric. Stitch outer colors again.

Optional: **Use a sewing machine to sew a satin stitch (1.5mm-2mm) around the edges of the design.**

School Symbol:
Use an original drawing of the school symbol and turn it into a stitchable design with the Bernette Deco Scan II.

• Trace school symbol (tiger paws) onto scanner paper.
• Set scanner with 5.0 density, color with satin stitch outline, 1mm wide.
• Scan the drawn outline of the design.
• Lay black construction paper over the design, leaving the alignment dot visible.
• Scan the design a second time (the screen will be black).
• Save the design to a memory card following the directions on the screen.
• Remove the card from the scanner and insert it into the embroidery machine.
• Hoop the cover fabric with Tear-Easy Stabilizer under it. Place Puffy Foam on top of the fabric within the hoop.
• Stitch the complete design (including outline) one time.
• Remove the hoop from the machine, but do not remove the fabric from the hoop.
• Carefully remove the excess foam. Reattach the hoop to the embroidery machine. Forward search to the outline of the design and stitch it again.

Sewing Construction Directions for the Cover

Note: Seam allowances used are 1/2".

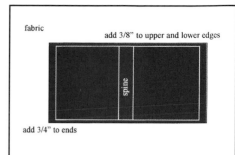

1. Open the binder flat over the embroidered designs and redraw perimeter lines if needed, adding 3/4" to each end (shorter edges) and 3/8" to the upper and lower edges.

2. Cut out the cover and back it with batting. Place the piping on stitching lines of the front cover, matching the raw edges. Using Bulky Overlock Foot #12 or #12C, and construction thread, stitch the piping in place, clipping the seam allowances at the corners.

3. Cut the inside cover the same size as the outside cover. Divide the inside cover into two pieces by cutting down the center of the spine area. Back these two pieces with batting. Turn the two cut edges under 1 1/4" and straight stitch to secure them.

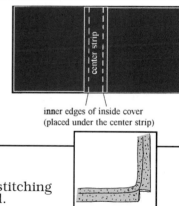

inner edges of inside cover
(placed under the center strip)

clip seam allowance of piping to turn corners

4. Cut a strip of fabric approximately twice as wide as the spine of the binder and as long as the cover. Finish the long edges of this center strip by turning each end under 1/2" and straight stitching to secure each end.

5. Lay the inside covers on the embroidered front cover, right sides together, matching the outer edges. Lay the center piece, right side down, over the inside edges of the front cover pieces.

6. Using the Multi-purpose foot, serge with construction thread around all four edges of the cover, sewing on the previous stitching line (piping). Turn the cover right side out, turning the center strip with one of the inside cover pieces. Insert the binder into the cover.

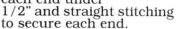

"Tigers"
A Liquid Sulky Solvy™ and Totally Stable™ Project

As shown by Joyce Drexler on the PBS TV Program "America Sews with Sue Hausmann."

by Carol Ann Ingram

Carol won first prize in the Wearable Arts category in a recent Sulky Challenge contest. This gorgeous outfit received numerous oohs and aahs as it travelled around the country for a year in the Sulky Challenge display.

"The liquid form of Solvy allows total fabric penetration to 'firm up' the more flimsy cottons. It also allows hooping for free motion without slipping in the hoop, and there is nothing to get in the way on the bottom during free-motion work. Totally Stable stays in place when you have to manipulate a more intricate design. It saves confusion and frustration with several layers." --- Carol

To make Carol's award-winning Tiger Ensemble you will need:

✔ **A Garment Pattern in your size that you will follow to construct the ensemble.** *(If you are going to make fringe, see Step 6 before cutting out that area of the pattern.)*

✔ **A Zig-Zag Sewing Machine, with free-motion capability and:**
  • Free-motion Darning Foot
  • Braiding Foot
  • Applique Foot
  • Tailor Tack or Fringe Foot
  • Cording or Beading Foot

✔ **Machine Needles:**
  • Jeans Needle and Top Stitching or Embroidery - Size 14/90

✔ **Sulky Threads:**
  • Sulky 30 wt. Rayon - 1055
  • Sulky Clear Invisible Thread
  • Sulky Original Metallic Threads -
    7001 - Silver, 7004 - Dark Gold
    7010 - Dark Copper, 7051 - Black
    7021 - Prism White
  • Sliver Metallic Thread 8051 - Black
  • Sulky White and Black
    Lightweight Bobbin Thread

✔ **Sulky Stabilizers:**
  • Solvy • Totally Stable

✔ **Coordinating Fabrics:**
  • Coarsely Woven Silk Tussah
  • Silk Lining Material
  • Tiger or Large Animal Print Fabric
    Carol used an Alexander Henry Print but any large animal print can be used.
  • Ultra Suede Scraps

✔ **Decorative Designer Yarns:**
  • "Forest Floor" Collection

✔ **Notions:**
  • 1 yd. Fusible Interfacing
    appropriate for fabric weight
  • 1/2 yd. Trans-Web
    paper-backed fusible.
  • 8 or 10" German made
    Hardwood Embroidery Hoops
  • Air or Water Erasable Pen
  • Fine-Line, Permanent-Ink Marker
  • Teflon Pressing Sheet or Press Cloth
  • Pin-Weaving Board
  • Sulky KK 2000 Non-Flammable
    Temporary Spray Adhesive
  • Small Sponge Brush
  • ScrapWrapper™
  • Assorted Beads & Fabric Glue

The raw silk fabrics chosen for this outfit are exquisite. It is a rich and beautiful outfit, perfect for the Goddess or the Tigress in you.

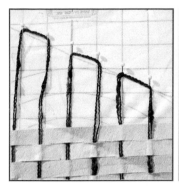

Step One: Ultra Suede Pin-Weaving
A. Cut pieces of fusible interfacing to match the sections on your pattern pieces that you have chosen to be the pin-woven sections. Pin the pieces of fusible interfacing, **fusible side up**, on a pin-weaving board. Cut scrap pieces of Ultra Suede into 1/2" strips slightly longer than the width of the area you are weaving. Using decorative yarns as the warp and the Ultra Suede as the weft, weave and pin sections for the back yoke, and separate sections for the front of the vest and the front of the skirt.

B. When weaving is completed, cover the pin-weaving with a press cloth or pressing sheet and steam heavily enough so the pin-weaving adheres to the fusible interfacing. Remove from pin-weaving board. Steam again from the back. Stay stitch around all edges to secure and stabilize them.

Step Two: Attach Pin-Weaving
To attach the pin-woven section to fashion fabric, lay it over the fashion fabric section that matched it. Pin an extra strip of 1/2" Ultra Suede over the seam and, using either Sulky Silver Metallic #7001 or Sulky Sliver Metallic or Rayon of your choice, do a decorative stitch over each edge of the joining 1/2" Ultra Suede pieces. This finishes the edge nicely and anchors the pin-weaving.

Step Three: Free-Motion Embroidery
A. To prepare the "Tiger Print" fabric for Free-Motion Embroidery, mix **Sulky Solvy** as directed on page 9 to make a liquid stabilizer, **except use about 1/3 less water** to make the solution stiffer.

B. Use a sponge-type paint brush to brush the liquid **Solvy** over each Tiger to be embroidered, extending the liquid **Solvy** out past the design to stiffen all of the fabric section that will be encompassed by your chosen hoop size. Hang to dry, or speed drying with a hair dryer.

C. Secure one stiffened section in an embroidery hoop and completely free-motion embroider over the Tiger with Sulky Metallic 7001, 7004, 7010, 7021, 7051, and Sulky Sliver 8051, using the fabric as your color guide. Hoop and embroider remaining Tigers.

Joyce's Tip:
Use more than one layer of Totally Stable if more stabilization is desired. Err on the side of more, rather than less. While it is easy to remove the stabilizer, it is almost impossible to get rid of puckers.

To avoid hoop marks on your Ultra Suede leaves, put a layer of Solvy over the Tiger and Leaf areas as you hoop them.

Step Four: Yarn Leaves
A. Use a disappearing or water soluble marker to draw a freehand outline of the large leaf on the garment either above, below or to the side of the tiger, or...if freehand drawing isn't your finest gift, trace the leaves on Solvy or Super Solvy with a fine-line, permanent-ink marker. Pin the Solvy to your garment.

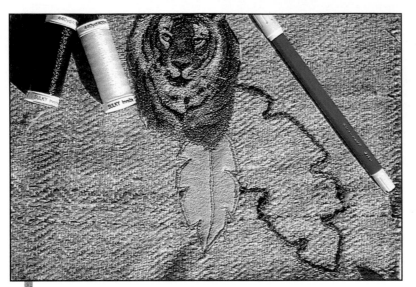

B. Using the cording or beading foot, couch down decorative yarns with Sulky Invisible Thread (clear for light yarns, smoke for dark yarns); use a blind hem stitch to allow the threads to "bloom" a little. A zig-zag stitch holds the fluffier threads too tightly to the fabric and doesn't allow them to "fluff".

C. Pull the Solvy away when finished. If any Solvy remains, spritz with water (if your fabric will accept water), and it will dissolve away. **Before applying heat**, remove the marks from the air or water soluble marker.

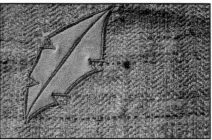

Step Five: Ultra Suede Leaves

A. To prepare the garment, use a <u>dry</u> iron to press Sulky Totally Stable onto the wrong side of the garment under the areas for the Tiger and Leaves.

B. Trace the Ultra Suede leaf design onto **Sulky Totally Stable** and press it onto the wrong side of the Ultra Suede. Cut out leaves. Peel off Totally Stable. Spray underside of leaves with Sulky KK 2000 Temporary Spray Adhesive and position them on the garment again and again until you are pleased with their arrangement. (Be sure to leave room for your Tigers.)

C. You may want some of the leaves underneath the Tigers and some overlapping the Tigers. If overlapping is desired, save some leaves to apply after the Tiger is appliqued on.

D. Use Sulky Gold Metallic #7004 to applique the leaves on with a small satin stitch.

Step Six - Applying the Tigers

A. After embroidering the Tigers, iron Trans-Web™ paper-backed fusible onto the back of each Tiger.

B. Cut out the Tigers leaving a 1/8" edge of fabric around them for appliqueing to the garment.

Step Seven - Making the Fringe

A. Make the fringe by initially cutting the garment longer than needed. Using a Sulky Metallic Thread, stitch a decorative stitch where you want the top of the fringe to start; this serves as a securing line to stop any fringing above that line.

B. Pull the threads of the fabric until it's fringed as much as you like. (On Carol's garment the fringe along the side of the skirt was prepared as a separate piece and inserted into the seam.) The more coarsely woven the fabric, the better its "fringing" ability.

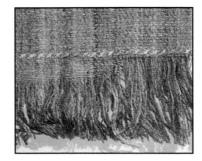

C. Position the Tigers where you want them on the garment and fuse them in place from the wrong side, using a pressing cloth or Teflon Pressing Sheet if your fabric is heat sensitive.

D. Rehoop one of the Tigers which are now on the garment. Using a straight stitch, free-motion stitch around the outside of the tiger, changing colors as needed. Follow the same procedure to finish the remaining tigers.

Step Eight - Making the Ultra Suede Flower

A. Cut the small flowers from Ultra Suede using either the Totally Stable method in Step Four or the Solvy method in Step Three.
B. For the "loopy thread" effect, use a Fringe Foot or Tailor Tack Foot (which has a bar down the center allowing the threads to be looser and fluffier) and Sulky 30 wt. Rayon Thread #1055, Tawny Tan to satin stitch around the flower.
C. Make the flower centers using wooden beads with tiny tassels made with the Scrap Wrapper and Sulky Metallic Threads which are then inserted and glued into the beads. Glue the beads to the centers of the flowers with fabric glue.

"Iris Garden" shown step-by-step in the book, DECORATING WITH THEME QUILTS and on the PBS TV Show - QUILTING IN THE HEART-LAND with Sharlene Jorgenson.

Self-Adhesive Templates

A Sulky Sticky™ Stabilizer Quilting Tip

Angela Jorgenson Scott
from Starbuck, MN

Angela has been quilting and teaching quilting for 10 years. She has lectured and held seminars around the country for Guilds and Quilt Shops as well as at Quilt Shows. She is a designer for QUILTING IN THE HEART-LAND and has appeared on many programs with her mother and Host of the program, Sharlene Jorgenson.

"Sticky Self-adhesive Stabilizer is ideal and a time-saver when making quilting templates since they can be reapplied over and over again as needed in repeated quilt blocks." --- Angela

Sharlene Jorgenson
Host of the PBS TV Show "Quilting in the Heartland"

Crazy Quilt and Vest as it was presented by Joyce Drexler on Sharlene's Program

Template Crazy Patchwork Angel Quilt and Vest

A Sulky Tear-Easy™ Stabilizer Quilting Idea

Sharlene has been quilting for 20 years. She has designed over 80 template patterns, stencils and even a flannel board for designing. Teaching all over the world, beginning at local quilt guilds and community education, she now reaches millions as the host of her own quilting show; QUILTING IN THE HEARTLAND.

" I find Tear-Easy Stabilizer to be the best foundation stabilizer for Crazy Patchwork by machine since it supports the decorative stitching no matter whether it is stitched in Sulky Rayon or Metallic Thread, and it does not tear out the delicate stitching when removed." --- Sharlene

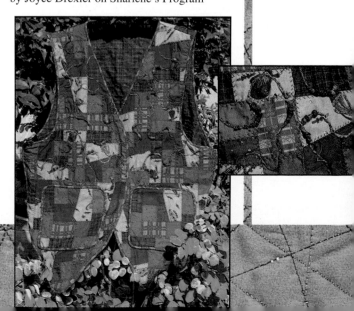

Sulky Lace Heart Embroidered Pillowcase

A Project using Sulky Solvy™ Water Soluble Stabilizer and Tear-Easy™ Lightweight Stabilizer for Heirloom Embroidery.

Martha Campbell Pullen

of Huntsville, Alabama

You will need:

✔ **Sulky Tear-Easy Stabilizer**
✔ **Sulky Solvy Stabilizer**
✔ Sulky 30 wt. Rayon Threads:
    1001 - Bright White
    1115 - Light Pink
    1108 - Lt. Mauve
    1077 - Jade Tint
✔ Sulky White Bobbin Thread
✔ 1/2 Yard of Swiss Batiste
✔ 2/3 Yard of 3/4" Insertion Lace
✔ 1 1/4 Yards of 3/4" Lace Edging
✔ 1 1/4 Yards of 1 3/4" Lace Edging
✔ 6" x 6" Piece of Organdy
✔ Starch
✔ Glass Head Pins
✔ #100 Wing Needle
✔ #60 or #70 Regular Machine Needle
✔ Stuffed Pillow - 12" x 16"

Martha is an internationally-known lecturer and author in the Heirloom Sewing field. She received a degree in speech and English and a Ph.D. in educational administration and management from the University of Alabama. Her love of sewing and children's clothing encouraged the opening of Martha Pullen's Heirloom Shop in Huntsville, Alabama, August 1, 1981. Two months later, she opened the wholesale division. She has presented workshops on French Hand Sewing by Machine throughout the United States, Australia, England and New Zealand. Books she has written and published include: *French Hand Sewing by Machine, a Beginner's Guide; Heirloom Doll Clothes; Bearly Beginning Smocking; Shadow Work Embroidery; French Sewing by Machine: The Second Book; Antique Clothing; French Sewing by Machine; Grandmother's Hope Chest; Applique Martha's Favorites; Heirloom Sewing for Women; Joy of Smocking; Martha's Sewing Room; Victorian Sewing and Crafts; Martha's Heirloom Magic* and *Martha's Attic.* Martha is also the founder and publisher of a best-selling magazine, *Sew Beautiful,* which is dedicated to heirloom sewing. She has just completed a television series for public television, entitled *"Martha's Sewing Room"*.

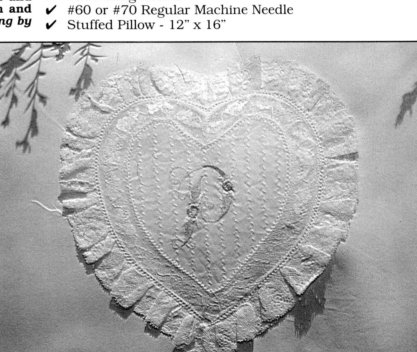

Instructions:

1. Cut a piece of Swiss Batiste 17 1/2" x 25". Starch and press. Fold the fabric in half to measure 17 1/2" x 12 1/2". Trace the lace heart template in the center of the lower half of the fabric.

2. Shape a 24" piece of insertion along the inside of the template lines to form a heart using the following steps:

    a. Place the pillowcase Batiste fabric on a fabric board (a board that can be pinned into and ironed on) or ironing board. Start at the bottom of the heart with a short lace tab extending beyond the template lines. Place pins at point "A" and "B". Pin the outside edge of the lace insertion along the template lines.

    b. At the upper point in the heart, place a pin at "C" and a pin at "D". Fold the lace back on itself and repin "C" through both lace layers.

c. Continue around the heart, pinning along the outer edge.

d. The inside edge of the lace will be floppy. Pull the very top thread in the lace so that the lace will lay flat against the fabric.

e. At the bottom point, where the lace criss-crosses, place a pin at "B" through both layers of lace. Flip the top piece of lace and pin through both layers at the bottom point. Starch and press. Repin the lace heart to the fabric.

3. Cut a piece of Tear-Easy larger than the lace heart

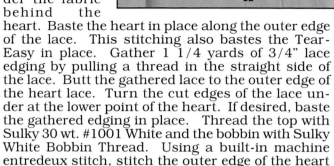

and place it under the fabric behind the heart. Baste the heart in place along the outer edge of the lace. This stitching also bastes the Tear-Easy in place. Gather 1 1/4 yards of 3/4" lace edging by pulling a thread in the straight side of the lace. Butt the gathered lace to the outer edge of the heart lace. Turn the cut edges of the lace under at the lower point of the heart. If desired, baste the gathered edging in place. Thread the top with Sulky 30 wt. #1001 White and the bobbin with Sulky White Bobbin Thread. Using a built-in machine entredeux stitch, stitch the outer edge of the heart and the gathered lace edging with a wing needle.

4. Carefully trim the fabric and Tear-Easy from behind the lace heart. Stitch the lace miters in place using a small zig-zag. Trim the excess lace tabs from behind the lace heart at the miters. Set pillowcase aside.

5. Put two layers of Solvy (one layer of Super Solvy) behind the square of organdy. Stitch rows of machine feather stitching 1/4" apart on the entire piece of organdy.

6. Put a piece of Tear-Easy under the organdy and stitch a machine monogram in the center of the organdy, making sure that the monogram fits within the heart opening. (Sample was done with Sulky 30 wt. #1115 Lt. Pink, #1108 Lt. Mauve, and #1077 Jade Tint.)

7. Pin the organdy square in place with the monogram centered inside the heart. Stitch the inside edge of the lace heart to the organdy using a wing needle, Sulky 30 wt. #1001 White, and a machine pin stitch (length: 2.5, width: 2.5).

8. Trim the excess organdy, Tear-Easy, and Solvy from behind the lace. Soak the pillowcase top in water to remove the remaining Solvy.

9. Cut a 25" piece of entredeux and 1 1/4 yards of 1 3/4" edging lace. Trim one fabric edge of the entredeux completely away. Gather the edging lace to fit the entredeux. Butt the gathered edging to the entredeux and zig-zag (length: 1.0, width: 3.0).

10. Place the entredeux/lace strip to the 25" side of the pillowcase, fabric edge of the entredeux to the cut edge of the pillowcase. Stitch the entredeux/lace strip to the pillowcase with a straight stitch that is placed next to the ladder of the entredeux. Trim the seam allowance to 1/8" and overcast the seam allowance with a zig-zag.

11. Fold the pillowcase in half, right sides together, matching the cut edges. Stitch along the two open edges of the pillowcase, using a 1/4" seam allowance. Overcast the seam allowance using a zig-zag or a serger.

12. Turn the pillowcase to the right side and press.

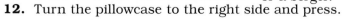

Miniature Applique Landscapes

A Sulky Totally Stable™ and Heat-Away Stabilizer Quilting Tip

Valerie Hearder
from Newfoundland, Canada

Valerie has been designing miniature landscapes since 1981. She exhibits and teaches internationally, and regularly at Houston's Quilt Festival. Valerie was included in Nihon Vogues' "88 Quilt Leaders of the World". Her inspirational book on miniature landscapes is called *Beyond the Horizon:* **SMALL LANDSCAPE APPLIQUE,** *published by C & T Publishing.*

"I designed and hand appliqued the landscape according to my 'cut and collage' method. I wanted to embellish the landscape with hand-dyed African leaf fabric and add free-form machine embroidery, but I wanted these two elements to be detached from the landscape, not stitched down flat. I basted the soft grey/green fabric 'hill' onto a double layer of Heat-Away for a firm foundation to stitch dense free-motion embroidery stitches that caught the edge of the "hill" fabric. I stitched the hill to the landscape, leaving the fringe stitches unattached and loose to add dimension and texture after the Heat-Away was disintegrated. Using fusible web, I fused the collection of leaves (9 separate pieces of fabric) into a single unit onto which I fused Totally Stable for added stability to stitch the vein details. The leaf unit was removed from the Totally Stable and secured to the landscape with a line of machine stitches along the bottom edge. The leaves were left unattached and 'floating' on top of the landscape, adding depth and dimension." --- Valerie

"Turned Edge Piecing"
Using Sulky Totally Stable™
Iron-On Stabilizer Tip

"I have been quilting for 20 years, but I had a difficult time working out techniques using tracing paper as a foundation. Luckily, Joyce Drexler solved my problem by suggesting I try **Sulky Totally Stable, Iron-on Tear-Away Stabilizer!!!** *WOW! What a product. I have used it extensively for over 5 years and I love it. It holds my turned edge pieces in place until I sew them, then I tear away the stabilizer and my piece is really flat and ready to quilt. For* **Passages** *I started with a photo, created a line drawing and 2 ghost layers: one of bricks and the ladder image repeated, and one of a color wash to determine colors not in the original image." --- Katie*

Katie began her art career in painting but quickly developed a talent for quiltmaking. Her work has gone from traditional quilts to three-dimensional, isometric perspective quilts. Her present work combines the organic quality of landscape with structure and geometry in her book FRACTURED LANDSCAPE QUILTS *published by C & T Publishing.* **Katie has been teaching since 1981.**

Fractured Quilt
"Passages" - 54" x 65"

Katie Pasquini Masopust
from Santa Fe, New Mexico

Photo by Hawthorne Studio

Midnight Magnolias

Jennifer Amor
of Columbia, SC

Jennifer designs "Classic Cutwork Machine Heirloom" patterns, patterns for bargello wall hangings and wearables, and the "Flavor Fun" series, which are patterns that teach children how to sew. She is the author of the book "Flavor Quilts for Kids to Make".

She teaches bargello, cutwork, wearables and surface design workshops nationwide. Her work has been published in books, magazines and calendars, and her quilt project for school children is funded in part by the National Endowment for the Arts.

You will need:
✔ **Sulky Solvy and Totally Stable**
✔ **Sulky Tear-Easy or Stiffy**

A 5-piece reversible machine cutwork garment creating 12 different "looks".

A Tear-Easy™ and Solvy™ Stabilizer Cutwork Tip

Jennifer's elegant Classic Cutwork designs by machine require several Sulky stabilizers and no hoop. To do the understitching, begin by applying Totally Stable (or liquid Solvy - see page 9 for instructions on making liquid Solvy) to the wrong side of the fabric. Use Sulky Solvy pinned underneath to sew the bars in the cutout areas.

To stabilize the fabric while embroidering the final design, add several layers of Tear-Easy or one layer of Sulky Stiffy Stabilizer (if the stitching is very fragile, Tear-Easy will pull away more gently, one layer at a time). Remove all stabilizers when the cutwork is completed.

Since most stabilizers are white, tiny white fibers often remain after stabilizers are removed. On white or light fabric, these are not noticeable, but on black fabric (or deep colors), they can ruin the design. Here's how Jennifer eliminates the "fuzzies":

1. Always use small, sharp scissors to cut away areas in the design.

2. BLOW away the bits--never brush them with your hand (you'll get MORE fuzzies!).

3. After removing stabilizers, use small scissors to CAREFULLY trim the white fibers from cut edges.

4. If any white fibers remain, make them vanish with a permanent fabric dye pen in a color that matches the fabric. (Be sure the ink is permanent on fabric.)

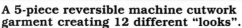

A Tear-Easy™ Quilting Tip

"Most of my machine quilting is done through two layers only: the shell, or outside layer, and the batting, and Tear-Easy is perfect for this, as it protects the feed dogs from the batting. Since I work with Wearables almost exclusively, and work with a mix of fabrics, it's great to know there is a Sulky stabilizer which can take care of any situation in stitching." --- Virginia

Virginia Avery
of Port Chester, NY

Virginia writes for many quilt, sewing and needlework magazines. She is also the author of: *The Big Book of Applique; Quilts to Wear; Wonderful Wearables: A Celebration of Creative Clothing; Hats: A Heady Affair; and Nifty Neckwear.* **In 1996 she received the Silver Star Award at the International Quilt Festival in Houston, TX.**

Stabilizer Do's and Don'ts

Before Sulky Stabilizers are marketed they are thoroughly quality tested in a wide range of applications that are common in both home sewing and commercial embroidery. Once they are introduced into the market, consumers often begin experimenting with using them in other diverse applications to achieve effects that were previously unknown. Often Sulky Stabilizers are combined with other products and/or techniques beyond what the stabilizers were designed for or intended to do. Most of the time the results obtained ranged from interesting to spectacular, and many of the people who discovered the better new uses were invited to submit the projects or ideas to be incorporated into this book and/or the prior "Concepts in Sulky Book Series".

*Occasionally, however, this experimentation has produced results that range from disappointing to disastrous. In the hope of preventing less than perfect results for others, on this page we will discuss some **Do's** and **Don't's** that will assure satisfactory results when you are using Sulky Stabilizers. Even though many of these are touched upon elsewhere in this book, we felt that having all of them together on one page would facilitate your understanding of them.*

TOTALLY STABLE

This marvelous product has a very light bonding material on one side that, when used properly, peels off and tears away very easily, and can be reapplied many times. Since Totally Stable is adhered by applying a hot iron for only several seconds, care must be taken when applying it to fabrics or fibers like **nylon or tricot that have a low melting point** which is very difficult to detect. If even the slightest melting occurs as you apply Totally Stable with a hot iron, when the fabric cools, some of the Totally Stable blends into and becomes part of the nylon; consequently, there is **no** way to remove all of it.

DO a test on a scrap piece to determine how much heat and for what length of time the receiving fabric can tolerate, to see if you can satisfactorily use and remove Totally Stable with that fabric. **DON'T** assume that the same heat setting on different irons produces the same amount of heat; some irons are much stronger than others. Also, if your ironing surface is already hot from recent use, you may need less heat from the top and/or a shorter time to achieve a satisfactory fusing of Totally Stable. **DON'T** iron Sulky Totally Stable onto fabric that has been marked with an air or water soluble marker since the heat could make the markings permanent.

SULKY CUT-AWAYS

When using Sulky Cut-Away Stabilizers under white or light colored fabric, **DO** trim close to the stitching to minimize stabilizer show-through.

HEAT-AWAY

When using Heat-Away in any project, **DON'T** expose the project to any liquid or moisture until the Heat-Away has been disintegrated with a hot iron. **DON'T** use a washable marker on the project because it has to be removed with water before a hot iron can be placed on it, since heat will make the washable marks permanent.

If Heat-Away is exposed to liquid or moisture, **DO** soak, agitate and flush any fabric that has come in contact with the project (this includes press cloths and ironing board covers) a couple of times in copious amounts of water to completely remove the chemical that causes Heat-Away to disintegrate; at this point, you can no longer remove the Heat-Away with a hot iron, it must be cut away.

Other Heat-Away **DO'S**: protect against moisture, heat and sun; store unused portions in a sealed zip-lock bag; embroidered designs where Heat-Away is not removed at once should also be stored in a sealed zip-lock bag.

SULKY STICKY

For best results when using Sulky Sticky, **DO** remove it from fabric within several hours of application. **DO** remove excess Sticky before applying heat from an iron or clothes dryer.

SOLVY/SUPER SOLVY

When doing long, time-consuming projects in a **dry atmosphere**, Solvy can become dry or brittle if the project is not stored in a sealed zip-lock bag between uses. One consumer whose Solvy became brittle after spending 40 hours of sewing over a 2 month period discovered that steam from a kettle of boiling water or a humidifier softened the Solvy for a short time so she could finish the project. Perhaps shooting it with a little steam from an iron may help.

To avoid having Solvy become overly limp in a **very humid atmosphere, DO** work in air conditioning and, between uses, store the unfinished project (and unused product) in a sealed zip-lock bag. Pressing Solvy with a dry iron at a low heat for several seconds will also stiffen it. In general, for greater visiblity, **DO** use a fine-line permanent-ink marker to trace designs onto Solvy. However, if Solvy will then be trapped under a heavy thread application of light colored thread on light fabric to the extent that it can't fully dissolve, a better choice would be a wash-out marker as long as you wash out the markings and dissolve the Solvy before applying heat.

DO look at each project as an individual, unique procedure and consider all of the properties of the fabric so you can choose the right Sulky Stabilizer to help you achieve fabulous results!